THE
DEMOTIVATED
EMPLOYEE

THE DEMOTIVATED EMPLOYEE

Helping Leaders Solve the Motivation Crisis
That Is Plaguing Business

CATHY BUSH, PhD
TARA PETERS, PhD

Published by Advantage, Charleston, South Carolina.
Member of Advantage Media Group.

ADVANTAGE is a registered trademark, and the Advantage colophon is a trademark of Advantage Media Group, Inc.

Printed in the United States of America.

10 9 8 7 6 5 4 3 2 1

ISBN: 978-1-64225-132-6
LCCN: 2019921158

Cover design by Matthew Morse.
Layout design by Matthew Morse.

This publication is designed to provide accurate and authoritative information in regard to the subject matter covered. It is sold with the understanding that the publisher is not engaged in rendering legal, accounting, or other professional services. If legal advice or other expert assistance is required, the services of a competent professional person should be sought.

Advantage Media Group is proud to be a part of the Tree Neutral® program. Tree Neutral offsets the number of trees consumed in the production and printing of this book by taking proactive steps such as planting trees in direct proportion to the number of trees used to print books. To learn more about Tree Neutral, please visit **www.treeneutral.com**.

Advantage Media Group is a publisher of business, self-improvement, and professional development books and online learning. We help entrepreneurs, business leaders, and professionals share their Stories, Passion, and Knowledge to help others Learn & Grow. Do you have a manuscript or book idea that you would like us to consider for publishing? Please visit **advantagefamily.com** or call **1.866.775.1696**.

CONTENTS

ACKNOWLEDGMENTS

We have been blessed to have many amazing and supportive people in our families, communities, and work lives. We are especially grateful to our friends, colleagues, and family members who have inspired us to take on this project, and who have sacrificed some of the time we would have spent with them while we were busy with our book. We are grateful for the many supportive people in our lives who kicked around ideas with us, previewed some part of our manuscript, helped us prepare for our promotional events and activities, and cheered us on during our journey.

It takes a village to raise a family ... and apparently to write a book. Some of the folks who were willing to go the extra mile to help us write our book included Tom Duncan, Donna Card-Sessoms, Susan Dennett, and Mark Bush, all of whom read our manuscript and provided helpful and candid feedback. Many thanks to Jatun Dorsey for sharing her wisdom about publishing and writing. Thanks also to those experienced authors and thought leaders who answered the call to provide endorsements of our book, including Barry Schwartz, Jim Kouzes, Scott Miller, and Ron Friedman.

We are very thankful to work with Nick Moon, who helped us build our assessment scale and conducted research in support of the leadership actions that we present in the book.

We are especially grateful for the many experts on our publishing team at Advantage|ForbesBooks. Ivy Hughes was a delight to work with, and her insights and creativity helped us transform our book from a "nerdy review" of demotivation to an interesting flow of ideas and examples that anyone can relate to and benefit from. Thanks also to our project manager, Rachel Griffin, as well as Josh Houston and the editing team, for working your magic with our writing, and for patiently teaching us about the various steps in the process of turning our manuscript into a book. To Caroline Nuttall, who helped us to successfully begin our publishing journey with our Blueprint Day, many thanks for your integrity and your guidance.

Our book is filled with stories that are real, although the names, jobs, industries, and sometimes genders have been changed. Whether you have been one of the leaders in our lives, or you have been a client or student who has shared a story about demotivation, we thank you all for teaching us about the various issues that people face in the workplace and inspiring us to offer ideas to help others who are facing demotivation issues and want to make some changes for the better.

Chapter 1:

WHAT HAPPENED TO THEIR MOTIVATION?

Amanda was a talented salesperson in a car dealership and recently completed a very intensive leadership development training program. She understood cars, people, and the importance of relationship building and was ready for the next step in her career. When Amanda was nearing the end of her leadership training, she approached the general manager at the dealership to see about being promoted to the job of used car sales manager and was immediately presented with a job offer. Amanda was excited about the job, and within no time at all, she was successfully leading her team of four used car sales folks.

Amanda always showed up to work with an amazing attitude and energy that was contagious. She hit the ground running, put in long hours, and was tirelessly committed to her work. Amanda's work style paired perfectly with the management style of her boss, who was very supportive, but saw no reason to micromanage Amanda. Amanda's boss gave her goals but didn't care how she got from point A to B. He let Amanda use her creativity to develop ideas that would build business for the used car department of the dealership. Before long, Amanda and her team had increased sales volume by nearly 20 percent and were receiving excellent customer survey feedback.

For two and a half years, things went well for Amanda and

the used car sales team. However, midway through Amanda's third year, the dealership was sold, and even though all of the employees were able to keep their jobs, they had a new general manager. This manager was very different from Amanda's former general manager, as he quickly established himself as aggressive and demanding, using condescending speech to get what he wanted from people. Amanda was frustrated with her new boss, but she loved what she did and felt obligated to the people in her department, so she stayed in her job.

Not long after the change in management, Amanda felt herself being micromanaged. She also noticed that she was the recipient of her boss's demeaning language. This type of behavior, of course, doesn't sit well with someone who's educated, knows their stuff, and has always been successful at their job. Within six months, Amanda left the dealership for a job as the new car sales manager at another dealership down the street. Within the year that followed, seven other people with different jobs in Amanda's former dealership found their way to her new one, and many of the customers found them at the new store as well.

The interesting thing about Amanda's departure was that her boss seemed to have no awareness of how his behaviors affected his employees, which ultimately caused Amanda to leave. Amanda didn't leave her job because she ran out of steam. Her motivation departed when management changed hands. Because her boss used language and actions that demotivated Amanda, the dealership lost a great asset.

There are far too many stories like Amanda's in workplaces throughout the world. The concept of motivation in the workplace has been studied for more than a century, yet it is still common to find employees who lack the basic motivation to effectively perform their jobs. Why is this still happening in the modern workplace? This is a question we sought to answer as we explored the continuing challenges faced by workers despite decades of research cautioning organizations and their leaders against the perils of demotivating employees.

As consultants and business professors, we have spent decades talking to people who struggle to improve their work lives and create great work environments for others. In the 1980s, Cathy worked in the marketing department for Dow Corning Corporation, a global chemical manufacturing firm. Nearly everyone in the firm had a technical background, and anyone who was deemed "high potential" had to do a quick rotation in human resources. At the time, Dow Corning had hired an expert in organizational development who was charged with developing more robust HR practices. Cathy ended up working with this expert to develop leadership training, which is how she found her passion—helping really smart, well-intended professionals trained in technical fields learn how to become strong leaders. One theme that came forth for Cathy was how frequently the leaders she worked with would mention their concerns about the lack of motivation of some employees on their teams. Cathy tucked this theme into the back of her mind, started her own consulting business in 1995, and returned to school in 2007 to get her doctorate in industrial/organizational psychology.

> "My interest has always been in helping leaders help others be successful, yet from the beginning, I knew we were on the wrong side of the motivation conversation. The conversation isn't how to motivate people, it's how do we stop doing things that demotivate them?"—Cathy Bush

While Cathy's first interest in the concept of demotivation came from her experience working with leaders at Dow Corning, Tara started digging into the research about motivation as she was studying leadership theory during her doctoral studies in educational leadership and systems. After spending almost a decade as an educator,

Tara returned to school to get her doctorate and became intrigued with how motivation impacts employees, leaders, and organizations.

> "I've always had this passion, love, and concern for people. Now I get to help working professionals understand that leadership is important in organizations. Research supports the impact that leaders have in organizations, and one of the consequential impacts leaders can have is how they create conditions that either motivate or demotivate people in a workplace context." —Tara Peters

While colleagues at Northwood University, we had regular conversations about employee motivation as a component of some of the articles and concepts that our students were studying, which is what led us to the topic of demotivation. Through these conversations, we began to recognize that the people we had been talking to about their leadership jobs don't wake up in the morning, stand in front of the mirror, brush their teeth, and say, "Okay, how will I demotivate people today?" Yet demotivation happens every day within every single organization. With *The Demotivated Employee*, we want to help leaders see things that they are doing to cause demotivation, and hopefully enable them to prevent demotivation from creeping in at all.

UNDERSTANDING HOW PEOPLE ARE MOTIVATED HAS A WIDE RANGE OF APPLICATIONS, FROM LEADING A SPORTS TEAM TO VICTORY, TO PARENTING, TO CREATING AN ENVIRONMENT FILLED WITH HIGHLY PRODUCTIVE EMPLOYEES.

Among a great many other topics, we find ourselves talking through the issue of motivation frequently with those we encounter. At least a dozen times a week, we end up in conversations with people about their workplaces. Usually, they want to discuss how their coworkers aren't motivated or what factors impact employee motivation.

Understanding how people are motivated has a wide range of applications, from leading a sports team to victory, to parenting, to creating an environment filled with highly productive employees. If only we could figure out the formula for how people are motivated, then we would be able to manipulate the variables in order to get them to behave in the most productive ways.

Perhaps you're thinking something like: "Oh no, not another book about motivation!" This would be a normal reaction, given that the topic of motivation has been vigorously examined by thousands of scholars and practitioners for more than a century and is part of the $15.5 billion leadership development industry.

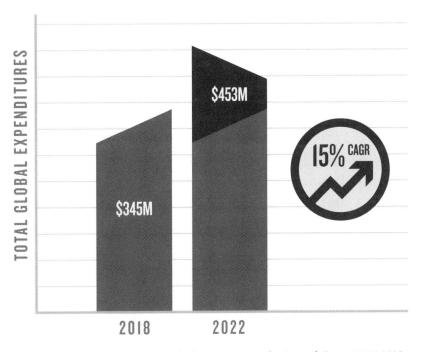

GROWTH IN GLOBAL MARKET SIZE OF LEADERSHIP DEVELOPMENT TRAINING EXPENDITURES

Source: Global Corporate Leadership Training Market Research Report 2018-2022

What makes *The Demotivated Employee* different from what we already know about motivation is that it is actually about *demotivation*, which would seem to be the flip side of the motivation coin. Demotivation is an area that isn't talked about as much as motivation. Although demotivation borrows from the literature and best practices on motivation, it actually starts from a different premise, which is that people come to us already motivated, and it is our job to keep them at least as motivated as they already were when they arrived for the task at hand.

It's not that managers are *trying* to demotivate their employees. Most managers are talented and intelligent and simply want to meet or exceed the goals that they have responsibility for. The challenge is that many of them are not trained and educated to understand the impact of their behaviors on others. Amanda's new boss didn't want her to leave, but his management style didn't allow him to understand how Amanda works, or what she needs from management to be successful in her job. This lack of awareness has a tremendous effect on the organization. When Amanda left, the dealership lost subject-matter expertise. The dealership also lost the continuity that comes with people who stay with the organization. Turnover is expensive. It costs money to train a new staff member. Teams have to reconstitute themselves, welcome the new team member, and get used to how they work. When a leader demotivates an employee to a point that they are forced to leave, the organization loses the continuity and cohesiveness that was in place for the team.

In order to understand the difference between motivation and demotivation, it is useful to understand the principles behind most existing theories of motivation. The first decision that a motivational theorist must sort through is whether they are dealing with a person's state, presented as a noun (motivation), or their behavior, presented as an action verb (motivating). This seems simple enough, but the difference is quite relevant to the lessons that one can learn from the theories presented. If you present ideas to managers, coaches, parents, and other leaders about the various ways that they can take action to motivate people, then your theories take on the perspective of motivating as a verb. It is an action (or set of actions) that people do unto others, producing responses to those actions. If you see motivation as a noun, then you acknowledge that it exists already within us, and you realize that ownership for the motivation belongs to the person themselves. This is an important distinction when we examine the concept of demotivation.

To see this comparison at work, let's take a look at a little motivation experiment one of our friends, Joanna, conducted with her sons when her oldest, Richard, was in middle school. When Richard, who had been a straight-A student, got to middle school, he decided he couldn't be both a good student *and* a cool student, so he let his grades slide. Panicked, Joanna devised a pay-for-grade scheme that she thought would motivate Richard to pull his grades back up. The scheme only paid Richard for As and Bs. So what did Richard do? He focused his attention on getting Bs. He actually got more Bs (and more friends) than he had ever had in a semester. It occurred to Joanna and her husband (after the experiment, of course) that Richard likely would have had better grades without the pay-for-grade scheme, because suddenly he got the message that Bs were okay (after all, they got rewarded). In an act of fairness, Joanna extended the pay-for-grade scheme to her younger son, Dallas, who had also always been an A student. With the scheme in place, Dallas had no trouble maintaining his As. Unlike Richard, Dallas's motivation for getting As was internal. He was happy to get the money, but it was not what drove his academic performance, which seemed to be about his own sense of accomplishment and pride. Richard's motivation was external. As soon as Joanna and her husband started paying him for his grades in school, Richard no longer felt the need to be responsible for his own motivation, because his parents took that over. Joanna's efforts for *motivating* Richard failed.

Much of the early research on reinforcement theories (Skinner 1969), social learning theory (Bandura 1977), goal theory (Locke and Latham 1990), and a wide range of other phenomena in behavioral psychology adopts the perspective that a person in authority can motivate another person with his or her actions. Our experience suggests that people come with motivation that is already present; however, another person can take actions that poke holes in that motivation, or demotivate that employee. Exploration of this idea began in the 1960s with the humanistic psychology movement. Following from scientific management principles, folks like Abraham Maslow started talking about motivation theory. McGregor was among the early scholars who began to challenge the idea of how we as managers see motivation in others, labeling this perspective "Theory X" (McGregor 1960). Theory X is the belief that workers come with zero motivation and will only be motivated by rewards and punishments in completing their tasks. Theory X also came to be known as the "Jackass Fallacy," using the analogy of motivating a donkey by offering him carrots when he performed in a desirable way and beating him with a stick when he did not.

McGregor also presented us with an alternative theory that examines the idea of motivation as a noun, or an internal state that exists within the person. He contrasted Theory X with Theory Y, which is a belief among managers that people come with their own intrinsic set of motivations, and our job is to help create an environment that maximizes their opportunity to achieve these. Intrinsic motivations facilitate a drive toward achievement, personal satisfaction, internal values, or a moral compass. These are not things that anybody else can give you. They are things that live *inside* of you. Your sense of worth, value, accomplishment, and achievement are all examples of intrinsic motivators.

Other scholars, including Maslow, also seemed to regard motivation as an internal state belonging to the employee. According to Maslow's hierarchy of needs, individuals have motivation that is based on their circumstances, and these motivations change over time (Maslow 1943). For example, when a person first enters the workforce, their highest criterion for selecting a job might be salary. But as they acquire more wealth and more family members—a spouse, children—their motivations change. Maybe they become more interested in being respected or spending time with their loved ones rather than focusing so much energy on making

> THESE ARE NOT THINGS THAT ANYBODY ELSE CAN GIVE YOU. THEY ARE THINGS THAT LIVE INSIDE OF YOU. YOUR SENSE OF WORTH, VALUE, ACCOMPLISHMENT, AND ACHIEVEMENT ARE ALL EXAMPLES OF INTRINSIC MOTIVATORS.

money. It is important to recognize that the motivation lives inside of the individual already and is not placed there by the actions of the manager (or some other person in authority).

The purpose of *The Demotivated Employee* is to examine what happens when a motivated person loses their motivation over the course of the time that they are performing the task. We refer to this as *demotivation*. This perspective relies on the premise that motivation is an internal state, although it also recognizes the way in which the manager impacts the motivational state of the employee, such that the behavior of the manager can serve as the catalyst for a reduction in motivation. We examine the idea of demotivation from the perspective of employees and their interactions with managers, although the concepts that we present are directly transferrable to other people completing a task and persons in authority (for example player/coach, child/parent, student/teacher). As you read through the ideas presented in *The Demotivated Employee*, you will likely find applications for these concepts across a wide range of roles that you have played and are currently experiencing.

We present motivation as a somewhat fragile state; that is to say, we believe people always start with motivation (otherwise they would not get out of bed in the morning), but their motivation at the beginning of a task may vary in strength and is easily influenced by the factors around them. Some of the factors will increase motivation, and some will have a demotivating effect. We have grouped these sources of demotivation into five categories. The typology is not meant to be exhaustive but is an evidence-based classification drawn from our review of the literature and professional experiences. The five sources of demotivation that we address in this book include individual differences, workplace stress, organizational culture, conflict between coworkers, and leadership style.

FIVE SOURCES OF EMPLOYEE DEMOTIVATION

Individual Differences

Stressful Work

Organizational Culture

Conflict Between Co-Workers

Leadership Style

We will go into these five sources in greater detail in Chapter 2. Considering these five sources, let's return to Amanda. By and large, Amanda left her position after being demotivated by the relationship between herself and management (source number five). Her boss had a coercive leadership style and, while that style might work for some people, it was really ineffective with Amanda.

As you consider the ideas presented in *The Demotivated Employee*, we encourage you and your management team to think about your employees and their motivation in this way. Imagine that your employees come to work with a basket full of motivation. These baskets may vary in size—some may be large, others may be small, but within each of those full baskets lies your employee's motivations. Your job as a leader is to keep that basket full. In *The Demotivated Employee*, we're going to show you what happens when one or more of the five sources of demotivation starts to poke holes in those baskets.

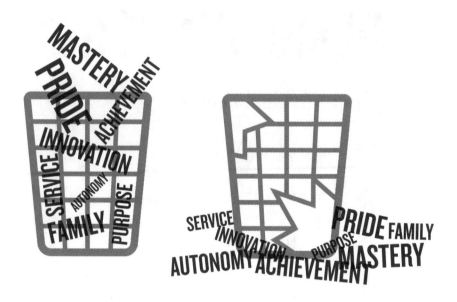

Each chapter of *The Demotivated Employee* offers an explanation of the various ways in which employees can become demotivated, supported by research and examples, as well as offering managers practical ideas about how to reduce the challenging practices and behaviors that might have the demotivating impact that is presented. At the conclusion of each chapter, we will provide a space for you to reflect on the ideas presented throughout the chapter so that you can identify your own strengths as well as areas of demotivation that you might improve upon.

Throughout *The Demotivated Employee*, we offer insight from scholars of leadership and management, as well as psychology, to help you understand how and why this topic is challenging and worthwhile to examine. To help illustrate the challenges, we provide examples from real people who have expressed issues with their demotivation, and we encourage you to apply your own examples along the way. Finally, we offer ideas for managers to consider that will help to reduce the negative impact on motivation, and invite you to reflect upon your own approach to managing and leading others.

We have helped thousands of leaders and students all over the world understand the impact demotivation has on employees, leaders, and organizations. In *The Demotivated Employee*, we will give you the tools you need to recognize demotivating behaviors that you and your leadership team might unintentionally be engaging in. We hope you will learn to look for these sources of demotivation on a regular basis as you work with employees, so that you can quickly address any issues that you see, and so that employees can quickly bounce back to being highly productive and engaged.

Chapter 2:

WHY DO LEADERS NEED TO SOLVE THE MOTIVATION CRISIS?

As a rising star at a large hospital in Texas, Harry loved his job. Within ten years, he had risen through the ranks of the hospital as a financial professional and, after several promotions, landed in a management role that allowed him to build patient accounts receivable systems that directly helped the hospital's patients, especially those who were struggling to pay their medical bills.

Harry was highly motivated and loved his work. He knew that he was making a difference and was always on the lookout for new opportunities that would improve the quality of his departments and grow the business of the hospital. He was well-liked and respected by his employees and peers, a fact that was reflected in his performance appraisals. Unfortunately, a casual conversation with a coworker placed the first puncture in Harry's basket of motivation.

During the conversation, Harry's colleague shared how, in an off-site meeting with other hospital leaders, a question had been posed about Harry's readiness for a new administrative role that would require increasing levels of responsibility and visibility. When asked for her input, Harry's boss, Sharon, had responded by saying that she didn't have confidence in Harry and didn't trust his judgment. Harry was blindsided by the comment, particularly because Sharon had never shared any concerns with him about his judgment. In fact, Sharon had always told Harry that he was doing a good job and that he was a valued employee. Furthermore, Sharon had never brought up anything in any of her reviews with Harry about his performance. During these appraisals, Sharon often praised Harry's work. Harry thought that he worked well with Sharon. Although she was demanding, she was approachable and supported Harry's initiatives. Or so Harry thought.

The following day, Harry showed up to work with a pit in his stomach. He wanted to know more about Sharon's opinion of him, but he didn't want to out the coworker who told him what Sharon said, so he sat at his desk silently. Frustrated and puzzled by Sharon's comments, Harry spent the day wondering what he could have done to cause Sharon to say such things about him.

Harry continued working for the hospital because a large part of his motivation was helping patients. However, his engagement level and commitment were significantly and adversely affected. He no longer volunteered for projects. He no longer spent his days walking from department to department checking on employees. He simply stayed in his office and did the bare minimum required to get through each day.

Think about the last time you started something new and the sense of excitement that you felt toward that endeavor. The morning you woke up for your first day on the job, you probably couldn't get out of bed fast enough. Your clothes were already laid out, your coffee smelled especially delicious, and every song on the radio was one you wanted to sing along to. You might have also experienced some fear or hesitation, but hopefully you found yourself looking forward to the new challenges with lots of positive energy and adrenaline pushing you toward the new task. That is the essence of motivation. Perhaps you are still doing that type of thing today, and you still get to experience that enthusiasm throughout every day; but for most of us, the level of motivation tends to change after the initial phase. For some of us, this can take months; for others, years. Sometimes our motivation drops due to new and more exciting challenges that replace the original. For example, someone might really enjoy working on a certain project, but feel their motivation lag once that project is completed. Often, we become demotivated by things that happen within the task that originally inspired our enthusiasm. Why does that happen to us, and why is it such a common problem? You are about to embark on a journey to explore this question, and hopefully learn how you can prevent demotivation among the people in your workplace.

Before going any further, let's start with an exercise. On the following page you'll find a checklist of leadership behaviors that may impact the motivation of employees (either positively or negatively). Place a checkmark by any of the behaviors that you do from time to time as a leader. If you are not in a leadership role, think about the behaviors that your own leader uses with you in your current role.

1. I reach out to talk with each of the employees who report to me about general topics in order to understand their various goals, values, and personalities.

2. I have a consistent style of leadership that is very predictable for employees across all types of situations.

3. The culture of the group that I lead gives people a lot of freedom and autonomy to complete their work.

4. I regularly discuss my perceptions about specific employees with other managers and employees who are impacted by their work.

5. I make sure that employees know that their input and ideas are welcome and create an environment where they can speak freely.

6. When I see two people who are struggling to work well together, I avoid getting involved in their drama, and expect that they will work out their differences.

7. When I can see that an employee is stressed out, I make time to talk through their issues and concerns and help them manage their stress.

8. I thrive on the excitement of changing processes and developing new procedures, even though I can see that it is taking a toll on others.

9. I make an effort to create cohesiveness among the people who work together in my department.

10. The culture of the group that I lead has a lot of structure, rules, and procedures, and I make sure to teach employees how to follow the hierarchy that is in place.

We will return to analyze the behaviors that you selected later in this chapter.

The motivation research is comprehensive and clear, detailing the drivers of intrinsic and extrinsic motivation and the factors that affect the levels of employee motivation at the group and individual levels. In his book *Drive: The Surprising Truth About What Motivates Us*, Daniel Pink cites the seminal research of Harry Harlow and Edward Deci (Deci 1971) regarding the drivers of human motivation and asserts that there's a "mismatch between what science knows and what business does" (Pink 2009). Barry Schwartz sought an answer to the question, "Why do we work?" and explored this question in his similarly-titled book (Schwartz 2015). Schwartz identified sources that contribute to worker satisfaction, and he lamented that for most workers, these attributes were missing from the world of work. This absence, in turn, had an adverse impact on employee engagement, which was linked to employee satisfaction, which was connected to employee motivation.

In fact, the 2017 Gallup report on employee engagement in the United States showed little change in the level of employee engagement from 2012 (Gallup 2017a). To be perfectly candid, the results are largely unchanged since 2000. Approximately 30 percent of the US workforce was engaged in 2017, meaning that employees "are involved in, enthusiastic about and committed to their work and workplace." Stated another way, 70 percent of the American workforce was NOT engaged. Why is this important? Well, this dismal statistic has financial implications for business. Gallup's research findings estimate that "disengaged employees cost the country somewhere between $450 and $550 billion each year" (ibid.). To understand how these costs relate to disengaged workers, we need to look at the three types of workers—engaged, non-engaged, and disengaged.

- Engaged workers work with passion. They feel a profound connection to the company. They drive innovation and move the organization forward.
- Non-engaged workers are checked out. They sleepwalk through their workday. They put time into their work, but they don't put passion into it (Harry).
- Disengaged workers aren't just unhappy at work. They're also busy acting out their unhappiness through devious behavior.

Returning to Harry, after hearing Sharon's feedback, he left the 30 percent and joined the 70 percent. Non-engaged and disengaged workers cost companies significant revenue by failing to do their work; wasting time rather than working; leaving, which forces the organization to hire and train new employees; and disrupting overall workplace morale.

The numbers provided by Gallup are staggering, and to compound matters further, the results of the 2017 Gallup *State of the Global Workplace* report found that up to 85 percent of employees are not engaged or actively disengaged at work. The economic consequences of this global "norm" are approximately $7 trillion in lost productivity. Eighteen percent are actively disengaged in their work and workplace, while 67 percent are "not engaged" (2017b). This latter group makes up the majority of the workforce—they are not your worst performers, but they are indifferent to your organization. They give you their time, but not their best effort nor their best ideas. This is exactly what happened to Harry. He was motivated and then he was demotivated by leadership. It's likely that most people come to work wanting to make a difference—but nobody has ever asked them to use their strengths to make the organization better, or their recommendations have been ignored.

The results from these studies confirm the idea presented by Dan Pink regarding the mismatch between what research is finding and what business is doing.

So we find ourselves wondering why managers are *unintentionally* demotivating their workforce. We're not cynics, so we don't believe this is intentional. We believe it is driven by our misunderstanding of or lack of attention to the issues of employee motivation and demotivation. Most managers and leaders have been groomed to recognize and assess the motivation of others, which is a very common aspect of leading people, but how many of us have ever thought about the factors that cause a motivated person to become demotivated? While the literature is replete with studies on motivation as noted in the previous discussion, the same is not true for demotivation. In fact, a review of the literature reveals very little scholarly work specific to demotivation, and a quick Amazon search reinforces the lack of publication on this specific topic.

Despite the limitations, we were able to find some relevant research that would be useful to our work. An article by Dean Spitzer (1995) is one of those sources.

While the article is more than twenty years old, the views expressed by Spitzer still resonate in today's workplace. He opens the discussion by describing a conventional workplace where employees are disengaged, off-task, and generally showing little initiative or interest in their work. However, he counters by stating that if you were

UP TO 85% OF EMPLOYEES ARE NOT ENGAGED OR ACTIVELY DISENGAGED AT WORK.

to engage in a conversation with these same employees, most would likely tell you this isn't how they want to feel about their work. They would like to feel the exact opposite. This is a motivational paradox.

It is likely that all of us can relate to the motivational paradox, and we just experienced it with Harry's story. On the one hand, Harry is able to find many activities in his job that match his values and skills and feel very motivating to him. His behavior shows demotivation after hearing that Sharon doesn't have high regard for his leadership skills, but he really wants to go back to loving his job again. This is Harry's motivational paradox. We tend to think that people in Harry's situation should simply "suck it up" and keep their focus only on the motivating stuff, but the holes in Harry's motivational basket are real, and it is hard to pretend that they are not there.

Additionally, in an article entitled "Work Is Not a Game," Robin Spencer (2013) posits the following:

> In the century since Frederick Taylor, Henry Ford, and Alfred Sloan invented the modern corporation, there has been an active production of research-driven literature about motivation at work; researchers have reached a general consensus on what motivates us. Herzberg and the huge Gallup studies on engagement capture the following key points:
>
> - Motivating factors and demotivating factors are not the same thing. For knowledge workers, for instance, money is not a strong motivator, but if it is perceived to be given unfairly, it can be a strong demotivator. In a manual labor space, money might be a much stronger motivation.
> - Perceived unfairness in policies and procedures is strongly demotivating. Fairness (or its lack) is recognized as a powerful force that may override economics in decision-making.

- The strongest motivator for knowledge workers is the belief that one's contributions matter, that they make a difference and serve a useful purpose. (Spencer 2013)

In the same spirit that Herzberg (2008) argued that dissatisfaction is not the opposite of satisfaction, we assert that demotivation is not the opposite of motivation. Demotivation is more complicated than this simplistic viewpoint, in part because the factors causing demotivation and motivation are distinctly different, as noted by Spencer. We will explore that distinction, and other related topics, in this book. But first, let's take a deeper look into the five sources of demotivation.

Individual differences include a wide range of things that we all bring with us to the workplace every day. These include factors such as an employee's inflated sense of competence and resulting frustration when the job requires more competence than they possess. There may be a mismatch between the employee's skills and the tasks, or between the employee's values and those of the boss, team, or company. We all vary in the type of commitment we bring to the job and the reasons why we are there, as well as carrying baggage about motivation from our previous experiences. There are dispositional factors, such as how positive we are, as well as personality factors. Finally, we all have different expectations and experiences with how much engagement we want in terms of decision-making and teamwork.

Of the five sources, this is the one source that is internal or attributable to the individual. The other sources of demotivation are external to the employee and can lead to demotivation because they also poke holes in the employee's motivation basket. Based upon our research, we recognize there are certain aspects of who we are, such as personality, that may cause us to be demotivated because of a mismatch between the work and the preferences of our personality, as an example. So, while this category focuses on the differences in each of the individuals who come to work, it is important for managers to understand these factors in order to avoid behaviors that create demotivation in employees.

WE ALL VARY IN THE TYPE OF COMMITMENT WE BRING TO THE JOB AND THE REASONS WHY WE ARE THERE, AS WELL AS CARRYING BAGGAGE ABOUT MOTIVATION FROM OUR PREVIOUS EXPERIENCES. THERE ARE DISPOSITIONAL FACTORS, SUCH AS HOW POSITIVE WE ARE, AS WELL AS PERSONALITY FACTORS.

Conditions of **workplace stress** can be very motivating for some people, very demotivating for others, and can vary in terms of the impact on people depending on the severity and duration of the stressors. Typical workplace stressors might include negative customer interactions, high pressure to perform to a certain standard or budget or timeline, a lack of predictability, or a highly competitive environment. Often these types of stressors can have a short-term motivational boost, but demotivation tends to creep in if they persist over a longer period of time or return frequently. Employees might also be demotivated by the stress of moral or ethical challenges, personal and professional sacrifices, and an imbalance between their personal and professional lives.

Employee demotivation can also be caused by the **organizational culture**, which includes processes, structures, and norms of behavior that employees must follow to complete their tasks. In very hierarchical organizations that offer employees little autonomy or opportunity for engagement, employees are most successful if they simply follow the rules and keep their mouths shut. This is a condition that can easily remove any motivation that they started with. In some organizations, the issues center more around ambiguity of values, cumbersome processes and procedures, or too much volatility and unpredictability, leaving employees confused about how to meet or exceed the organizational expectations. Employees expect to be treated fairly and with transparency when it comes to systems that impact their compensation and promotion opportunities, and can be highly demotivated by these human resource processes and the overall sense of a lack of organizational support. Unless they are a part of the executive team that creates the organizational culture, structure and processes, most managers feel helpless in addressing the issues caused by the organization, and this helplessness only serves to further demotivate the employees.

Conflict between coworkers can be a demotivating source for employees. When you gather a bunch of people together, you will inevitably experience relationship conflict, which may range from workplace incivility to bullying and harassment. We bring our own biases to work, which can negatively impact our ability to work with others, and we also bring a certain emotional energy to work that can be very contagious, especially if our energy is negative. Peer communication and feedback processes can be useful in minimizing many of these issues for workers. However, these processes may also be set up in a way that demotivates workers. Managers play a key role in establishing highly productive norms to avoid this negative impact on motivation within teams.

Leadership style in the workplace also plays a role. Demotivation can be a result of a lack of trust in that relationship, or an absence of clarity about the meaning or purpose of work. If the leader provides infrequent or ineffective feedback, or a lack of clear direction, the employee's motivation may be impacted. Most employees need some coaching and support from their leader, but not all leaders recognize that need or have the time or skill set to deliver these effectively.

Managers and leaders often have very busy and challenging jobs, and therefore may not communicate or interact with their employees very often; they may ignore or disregard employees' work, or only notice errors and place too much emphasis on critique. Some leaders fail to take action, either because they lack organizational power or take a conservative risk posture, which may lead to missed opportunities for the department or organization as a whole. Many of these behaviors are accounted for in the concept of leadership styles. We will examine the different behaviors of leaders as they relate to motivation of employees, with the intent to remove those behaviors that are demotivating.

Now that you've read Harry's story and understand a bit more about the five sources of demotivation, it's a good time to return to the results of the leadership behavior self-assessment that you completed at the beginning of the chapter. Which of these behaviors did Sharon use in motivating or demotivating Harry? The odd-numbered items are all behaviors that should prevent or reduce the demotivation of employees such as Harry. Did you see Sharon using any of these? It appears likely that Sharon used behaviors one and three, and maybe even five, or so Harry thought. These behaviors probably helped Harry's motivation leading up to the most recent events. Sharon also used one of the behaviors that can lead to demotivation, which was behavior four—talking about Harry behind his back. In fact, all of the even-numbered items in the checklist are leadership behaviors that demotivate employees.

Perhaps at one point in your career, you could have related to Harry. The purpose of this book is to get you to think about Harry's manager, Sharon, and what she might have done to change the behavior that contributed to Harry's demotivation. Take a moment to think about a challenge you've had with an employee. Then retake the quiz, applying it to that situation. While the exercise isn't scientific, it can provide a window into your behavior, or your boss's behavior, and the impact on employees. If the results weren't as favorable as you'd like, don't worry. That's why we've written *The Demotivated Employee*.

REFLECTION:

Take a few moments to consider the five sources of demotivation. Choose two that you believe may be impacting some of your employees and write them down below.

_____

_____

_____

_____

_____

_____

FIVE SOURCES OF EMPLOYEE DEMOTIVATION

- Individual Differences
- Stressful Work
- Organizational Culture
- Conflict Between Co-Workers
- Leadership Style

Chapter 3:

INDIVIDUAL DIFFERENCES: UNMOTIVATED WORKERS NEED NOT APPLY!

Cathy loves going on cruises in part because she gets to talk to the staff. In fact, by the time the cruises are over, Cathy knows the staff quite well. She learns about their lives, why they decided to join the cruise ship, and what they want for their futures. These relationships develop because when Cathy asks cruise ship employees about their jobs, they go on and on about how much they love their work, traveling, and meeting new people.

A few years ago, Cathy was on a cruise around the Hawaiian Islands. As she always does, she asked one of the servers about her job. Instead of smiling and sharing the things she most liked about working on a cruise, the woman said, "I work so hard. In fact, this is the hardest job that I've ever had. There are so many rules—we even have to share a room with another person—and I'm lonely all the time."

By the end of the first day on this cruise, Cathy's family had all mentioned that they got variations of the same response. Most of the people working on the ship seemed to be miserable. They didn't like their jobs and thought they were overworked and underpaid, and their attitudes showed it. Not only did it take a concerted effort for them to smile, but they also walked quickly past guests that were clearly seeking help, acted irritated whenever someone approached them, and seemed to disappear whenever any guest needed them.

So what happened? Why were so many of Cathy's other cruises full of friendly employees who were clearly motivated, and her trip to the Hawaiian Islands not? Why is it that some people seem to readily demonstrate their motivation, and others look like they would rather be anywhere but at work? As we begin our examination of the five sources of demotivation, we will discuss individual differences that represent the ways in which employees are distinctly diverse. One of the key differences we need to explore are personal, internal factors. Personal factors may be related to:

1. An employee's sense of competence.

2. A mismatch in expectations between the employee and their manager.

3. Other attitudes and dispositions, such as personalities or commitment.

When we observe highly motivated people, we tend to think that they were born that way (and the same is true when we observe unmotivated workers). However, we all bring personal factors to work with us, and they play a very important role in how we process the wide range of work activities that we experience, and whether these activities inspire or destroy our motivation.

To illustrate these three personal factors, we will examine several small examples of workers in different situations.

SENSE OF COMPETENCE

When an employee feels that they are in over their head, their motivation may be affected. This is considered a competence-related issue. That's exactly what happened to Lois, a clerk at a boutique hotel in Singapore, who was absolutely thrilled to start her new job. On the first day of work, Lois arrived happy, smiling, and eager to learn new skills. As she walked through the lobby, she smiled at every guest and made eye contact with each employee. As she went through the training process, she asked good, engaging questions. For weeks, Lois even showed up to work early.

But as time wore on, Lois was asked to take on more and more responsibilities. One day, after very little training, Lois's boss asked her to start using a new guest registration system that had recently been introduced to the hotel. This made Lois very nervous. She did not want to be responsible for making scheduling errors that could dramatically and negatively impact a guest's experience. While Lois was learning the new registration system, her boss started leaving her alone at the desk for long periods of time. He felt that because Lois had completed her training, she should be able to handle anything that came her way. However, Lois found that she often came across activities that she had not faced during her training, and when she turned to ask for help, no one was there to answer her questions.

Within a three-week period, Lois's enthusiasm for her job changed dramatically. When she interacted with guests, she had to force a smile. When she walked through the lobby, she barely made eye contact with anyone. Instead of showing up early for work, Lois started calling in sick when she knew her shift would entail long periods of time alone at the desk. Lois never told anyone that she was struggling with the new guest registration system. She was afraid that if she did, she would be fired, so she tried to fake her way through it.

Three months after feeling on top of the world about her new job prospect, Lois handed in her resignation.

Lois's challenge with her job was primarily driven by a concern about her competence level and skills. This concern is a *normal response* for an employee to have, especially when they first start a job or are learning a new skill. When we are in training, we may have some motivational challenges associated with our competence, but we typically see the opportunity to learn something new as a motivating process. This is especially true if we work in an organization where it is regarded as "normal" to be a learner and not an expert all of the time. Once we are expected to have mastered a skill or task, it can be very frustrating to bump into obstacles, and this can often have a demotivating effect on people. If a person has some baggage from a prior work experience, this phenomenon will be magnified out of fear that the same negative thing might happen again in the new situation.

In Lois's case, that baggage came from her experience at a different hotel. At that hotel, every time Lois asked for help, her boss ridiculed her and made her feel stupid. Lois's boss at her new job didn't know this, of course; yet this personal work history caused Lois to stay quiet when she felt she still needed support. So, we believe it's important that managers know and understand that feelings of incompetence are a real obstacle for employees, and that if they're not overcome, employees, like Lois, will leave the organization.

MISMATCH IN EXPECTATIONS

An additional personal factor that can lead to demotivation is misunderstanding the expectations that others have for us, as compared to our own expectations. We refer to this as the *psychological contract*, or the unspoken expectations that exist between people and their organization, or between coworkers (Zhao et al. 2007). This psychological contract is "signed" before anyone becomes an employee of a company. When we apply for a job, we have some expectations about what the job is going to entail, what we're going to have to do, the kinds of things that we will be responsible for, and what the company is going to be like. This continues through training and then begins to shape how we actually approach our employment.

In the case of Lois, she may have expected to get a lot of help with the new system. Or she may have expected that she would never be left at the desk alone, and therefore would not have to figure out difficult things with customers on her own. It may be that she had expectations about her own ability to learn something new, and she was frustrated when she fell short of her own expectations for herself. If these were her expectations, then her motivation would naturally drop once they were violated.

The *psychological contract* is a two-way street that exists between the employee *and* the manager. When a manager interviews a job candidate, they make assumptions that then create expectations. Perhaps Lois's boss talked to her about her previous experience working for a boutique hotel in another city. Based on that information, maybe he assumed Lois would have no trouble handling the new reservation system and, given that he had no knowledge of her previous experiences, there was no reason to adopt another view.

Not only can missed expectations develop before a person starts a job, but they can also come from a variety of sources, as we all have likely experienced in our work lives. Think back to a time when you had an expectation about how you might contribute your ideas to a new work project or goal, only to find out that your ideas were never sought, or someone else got credit for your idea. Perhaps you have had an experience in which you imagined the way that various members of a team were going to work together, only to find out that your teammates did not follow the expectations you had at all, and left you waiting for things that you needed them to complete. These types of missed expectations may be so common that you have learned not to be frustrated by them. But it is likely that at some point in time, your motivational basket had a hole punched in it because of these challenges.

ATTITUDES AND DISPOSITIONS

Another category of personal factors that may impact demotivation in employees is our *attitudes and dispositions*, the tendencies that people have to respond to situations in ways that are predictable or consistent (Judge et al. 1997).

Dispositions can include attitudes as well as behaviors associated with our personality. These dispositions tend to be easily spotted when watching an employee performing his tasks at work. Although a person might try to conceal them, we can usually tell who loves their job and who hates it. Loving your job comes down to three factors:

- Personal affect
- How well your job fits your personality
- Your sense of commitment to the job
  (organizational commitment)

Personal Affect

If you've ever watched or read "Winnie the Pooh," you've experienced a nice dose of two contrasting affects. Tigger, the rambunctious, upbeat tiger, is a character who has an abundance of positive affect. Eeyore, the gray, grumbly donkey who's always complaining about this or that, clearly demonstrates his negative affect.

Affects aren't just for cartoon characters. They impact all of us. Each of us has an *affect* that informs our outlook and approach to various situations. Although our affect can vary, it tends to be quite stable across a wide range of situations. A person with *positive affect* tends to look at the world with optimism, sees the positive in past and present situations, and is hopeful about the future. This person points out the good in the things that he or she experiences and tends to spread that positive energy to others. Conversely, a person with *negative affect* has a gloomier view of the things that he or she experiences, and likely has thoughts and behaviors consistent with a pessimistic or negative view of the past, present, and future. Most people carry these dispositions across all aspects of their lives. If they're positive at home, they tend to be positive at work. If they express themselves negatively at work, they'll do the same at home.

There are nonverbal cues for a person with a positive affect, including smiling and friendly body language, which seem to be absent from people who have a negative affect. This basic disposition allows us to recognize the motivational state of others, as we tend to use the body language and verbal cues of positive affect to indicate a high level of motivation, while correlating negative affect with demotivation. Being around a person with positive affect can help us to be more motivated as well, and conversely, we can lose motivation when we hang out with someone who shares their negative affect in our environment.

In a work situation, the contrast between affects is often stark. Richard and Shawn were coworkers in an accounting firm. Both started at the same time and had attended new employee orientation where, in a true story of opposites attract, they struck up a friendship. Richard was happy-go-lucky and an eternal optimist. His glass was always half full no matter the circumstances. Even when the firm was undergoing layoffs, Richard was able to see the silver lining. He even referred to the layoff as an opportunity. Richard's outlook was always positive and people tended to gravitate toward that. He was just that kind of person. Shawn was the polar opposite. He was always complaining, he never looked for the silver lining, and his glass was always half-empty. If the company gave everyone a $20,000 raise, while everyone else celebrated, Shawn would say, "It should have been $25,000. Why didn't they give us that?" Shawn was always negative, something was always wrong in his life, and he always saw the potential downside to every situation. Because Shawn was so consistently negative, his coworkers tried to limit their interactions with him. Of course, Richard tried to go to bat for him, saying "Ah, he's not really that bad." But the others would say, "Look, every time you go around that guy, he's like a buzz saw. He kills the atmosphere in a room because he's so negative."

When people would ask Shawn why he was so negative, he would say, "I don't know. It's just the way I am." Richard and Shawn are the perfect contrast between a positive affect and a negative affect.

It's important to note here that a person who has positive affect *looks* motivated. That doesn't mean that they are. It doesn't mean that they don't get demotivated. People with a positive affect will bounce back pretty quickly from a demotivating situation because they're going to put the positive spin on it, but that doesn't mean that they don't also feel demotivation. A similar scenario exists for people who have a negative affect. Just because someone has a negative affect and constantly complains about their job doesn't mean that they're demotivated, although the tendency is to think that's the case. They may not be demotivated at all. They just approach the world from a grumpy place. Sometimes managers only look at affect to determine motivation, which can lead to a limited and inaccurate understanding of their employees.

Most people learn to have the affect that's expected in their workplace, and so many people learn to mask their affect. Masking an affect comes from setting aside where you normally are to be where you think you're supposed to be. When someone masks their affect in order to maintain employment, they tend to learn to have the affect that's required. For example, if you work for a collection agency, they probably don't want you to be positive, optimistic, and bubbly in everything you do. In fact, the normal behavior within your workplace might be skepticism because that behavior helps the teams collect debts. In this situation, someone with a positive affect might have to mask it. While we might assume that negative people are the ones who have to wear a mask at work, depending on the company culture, a positive person might have to do the same.

> MANY OF THESE PERSONALITY CHARACTERISTICS RELATE TO MOTIVATION AND DEMOTIVATION, SO IT IS USEFUL TO CONSIDER WHERE THIS COMES FROM, AND HOW WE MIGHT HELP A PERSON MAXIMIZE THEIR MOTIVATION BY EMPHASIZING (OR MINIMIZING) THE RELEVANT PARTS OF THEIR PERSONALITY.

Personality

None of us would be surprised by the statement that each person has a unique combination of *personality* characteristics that contribute to his or her behavior at work. Many of these personality characteristics relate to motivation and demotivation, so it is useful to consider where this comes from, and how we might help a person maximize their motivation by emphasizing (or minimizing) the relevant parts of their personality. Although individuals can develop behaviors outside of their personality, it has been argued that personality is largely a fixed characteristic that is inherited, and therefore should give very useful information about individual differences in behaviors that lead to motivation. Using the Big Five Personality Trait Model developed by Costa and McCrae (1992), we can dissect the way in which an individual's personality may contribute to their demotivation. The Big Five Personality Trait Model theory includes the following personality characteristics:

- Extroversion
- Agreeableness
- Emotional stability
- Conscientiousness
- Openness to experience

Extroversion

Although extroverts and introverts can all be motivated and also demotivated, the place where it is relevant to consider this element of personality is with the idea of fit for a certain job. When a person is introverted by nature, she prefers to work with thoughts and ideas rather than with people, may prefer solitude for her work, and is likely to feel smothered by activities that require a great deal of interaction with others, which could become demotivating. Likewise, a person who is extroverted gets a lot of energy from others and finds teamwork motivating, and would therefore be frustrated if expected to work alone for a long period of time.

Years ago, Cathy worked with a guy named Brad who is a perfect example of the impact of this aspect of personality on motivation. When Brad was hired to work as a formulator, he was excited by the opportunity to work in a state-of-the-art laboratory, to experiment and design, solve problems, and to work alongside many other brilliant chemists. Because Brad was working on new product development that had the potential to be a significant breakthrough in the industry, he was given all of the equipment and space he needed to work, with his own office area that was isolated and the freedom to work a schedule that provided him with a lot of time to think and work on his own. Occasionally, he was asked to present his findings to a group of his peers, which he liked quite a lot because he was highly respected within the company. From time to time, he was invited to meet with marketing, sales, and purchasing professionals from other organizations. This made him a bit uncomfortable, but he accepted that he needed to help others understand the work he was creating, so he managed to be impressive for those types of activities as well.

Based on his great track record, Brad was eventually asked to lead a team of chemists who worked more directly with the customers who were formulating new products using the chemical compositions that he had developed. Within this new project, the time that Brad spent in customer and business meetings increased significantly. The project also included lots of new activities that required him to provide feedback, coaching, and support to the other people on his team, which sometimes made him uncomfortable. All of these activities cut significantly into the time he had available to work in his lab, which he missed very much. He found himself exhausted at the end of each day, having spent all day interacting with others, and getting no time to think or experiment. Although he had the respect of his peers and the organizational leadership, and a bigger paycheck, he found himself longing to return to the isolation of his lab.

Like many of us, Brad had found himself in a job that matched his introverted and analytical personality, and then his job responsibilities changed, which put him in activities that were not a great fit with his personality, causing a major shift in his motivation.

Agreeableness and Emotional Stability

The personality characteristics of agreeableness and emotional stability have a more direct impact on the construct of demotivation. People who are agreeable might be the least likely to become demotivated, because they are simply happy to go with whatever is asked of them, and they don't demand much from the situation other than an agreeable environment. An agreeable person tends to be good-natured and cooperative. Agreeable people care about the people they're working with, they try to work well with others, and getting along is important to them. Similarly, people who are emotionally stable tend to be calmer, less sensitive, and not prone to feelings of negativity. Because of their optimism and reduced levels of anxiety, they're better able to respond to stressful situations. As a result, emotionally stable individuals are less likely to be demotivated.

People who are low on the trait of emotional stability are more prone to slip into a state of demotivation, as they are likely to be uncomfortable and find reasons to be concerned about nearly every situation. Issues with emotional stability are often hidden until organizational challenges arise. When change happens, people often feel worried and threatened. The degree to which they feel these emotions determines their emotional stability. Let's say the corporate headquarters of a large manufacturer is moving from one facility to another. Let's see how Sarah, who is agreeable, and Bob, who is not so agreeable, might approach this situation. The day of the move, Sarah packs up her stuff, ready to go to whichever office she's been assigned. Bob, on the other hand, complains to his manager about the bookcase in his office. It's too small, it doesn't look like the one he used to have, and he doesn't like the distance between each shelf. For the period of time that they are planning for and implementing the move, Bob's motivational basket is filling with holes, while Sarah does not seem to be experiencing any demotivation associated with the move.

Conscientiousness

Conscientiousness refers to how conscientious employees are of their coworkers and team members. So, a person either values follow-through on commitments, reliability, and predictability, or they prefer to be spontaneous and unpredictable.

Years ago, Cathy was working with a team of professionals from around the world who were launching a new global marketing campaign. As such, she worked on a team with people in China, Germany, and Brazil. Due to the geographic difference, conference calls always occurred at strange times of day. Near the end of these calls, the team would develop an action plan that covered the agreements made in the meeting, along with the follow-up actions for each team member.

Several of the team members would write follow-up notes. It was common for people to get their tasks done ahead of time, copy the rest of the team on their emails, and offer their point of view on any conflicting issues. The majority of the team was really considerate of other members; however, two people on the team never said anything. They read the emails and the comments, but never replied to the emails, and it was rare for either of them to finish their tasks by the next meeting as agreed upon. Instead of coming to the meetings with their work, they arrived with an excuse as to why they hadn't finished on time. As a result of their lack of conscientiousness, the rest of the team started to work around them and eventually began communicating separately and filling in the two nonparticipating team members. The two became even less motivated to contribute, and the rest of the team was demotivated based on the extra work that they had to do to get things done. Although the project was completed successfully, the experience was demotivating for nearly every member of the team.

Openness to Experience

Openness to experience relates to the willingness of individuals to be open-minded, to take risks and to experiment. Individuals who demonstrate an openness to experience are more likely to try new things, question the status quo and be comfortable with failure because of their willingness to experiment.

Over the last five years, Tara has worked as an international consultant on micro-businesses in Sri Lanka and India. This work has focused on helping those living at the bottom of the pyramid (about four billion people living on less than $2.50 per day) to create businesses that would result in a new future for themselves and their families. One of the first hurdles in this work is opening the eyes of those participating in the project and encouraging them to not only see new possibilities but try something new. One example was a nonprofit in Coimbatore. The director was looking for a way to create a micro-business that could provide financial resources to support operational needs for programs that served the indigent. After meeting with the director and staff, it was decided that a goat business would be started. The nonprofit had never tried anything like this; in fact, they had never even thought about owning a business. But the director was open to the idea of change. So, after a week of consultation and the development of a preliminary business plan, the first kid was purchased six months later. After being in business for less than twenty-four months, the new goat farm was profitable, and the organization had sufficient resources to fund new programs. Plans were underway to start a second micro-business in a local village. In a follow-up discussion, the director commented that he was so motivated by the chance to do something different that could really help the nonprofit pursue its mission and make a difference. In contrast, someone closed to experience would have been unlikely to have tried the goat farm.

Most of us can remember a work experience in which a new opportunity was presented. We make the choice whether to pursue that opportunity or not. That decision comes with risks. Those who are closed to experience find new opportunities very frustrating. The more pressure they are under to pursue new opportunities, the more demotivated they become.

Organizational Commitment

Organizational commitment is a very specific type of disposition that impacts our motivation (and demotivation). It is usually a construct that applies to a person's relationship with their job rather than with a specific task that may or may not be motivating to them, which makes it an interesting factor to consider. In the organizational commitment model developed by Allen and Meyer (1996), there are three types of commitment that a person may have toward their organization, including affective, continuance, and normative commitment.

- *Affective Commitment:* A person who displays affective commitment has a strong loyalty and deep concern for the organization, its welfare and mission, and the people in it.
- *Continuance Commitment:* Continuance commitment comes from a belief that the employee cannot afford to leave the organization, often based on salary or specific benefits that allow him an opportunity to meet some other goal in his life. In this form of commitment, the employee often sees himself as a "prisoner" in a job that he doesn't necessarily love, but cannot leave.
- *Normative Commitment:* Normative commitment is based on a sense of obligation, such as a belief that the organization won't be able to meet its goals without your specific expertise. This sense of obligation may provide a source of pride, but also can cause an employee to feel trapped.

Although a person's organizational commitment may be dynamic enough to change in different situations, it is likely based on an attitude or choice that the employee makes, not necessarily the behavior of others. A person with affective commitment is likely to maintain a high level of motivation and to successfully fight through any factors that decrease motivation, because of their strong loyalty and deep concern for the organization overall. Those who work with continuance or normative commitment may be more susceptible to bouts of demotivation, due to the external source of motivation that they are already experiencing, and the instability that is presented by these kinds of external sources.

Let's look at what these types of commitments look like in a real working situation. Cathy once worked with a large printing organization. Right before the third shift, a line of about seven people got together for a meeting about that day's work, which included producing an environmental magazine. Brian, who had an affective commitment, said, "How cool is this? We're printing a magazine that's going to help people in the community improve water conditions and change lives." This response was typical of Brian, who always took the time to learn about any new project. For Brian, it was always important to understand why his work mattered in a larger context. Outside of work, Brian proudly wore the company's T-shirt and was always quick to tell people how much he loved his job. Bryce, who had a continuance commitment, nodded his head and did his best not to roll his eyes about the project. "Will we get paid more for this project?" he asked the line manager. Bryce's first son had just started college and his wife had a modest-paying job down the road. Between his wife's job and tuition payments, Bryce felt stuck in his current position. Steve, who had a normative commitment, didn't say much during the meeting. He had been with the company for ten years and was experiencing burnout, but didn't say much unless asked specifically about his job, which he knew he could do well. Even though Steve didn't like that his hours had changed over the years and that he felt less valued, his commitment to doing what he could for the company was strong. He often thought to himself, "Things will fall apart if I leave."

Although there are many things that we do as managers and leaders that impact the motivation of workers (as highlighted in many other chapters of this book), some of the issues that employees face are directly caused by the types of personal factors that have been described in this chapter. As a boss, it is very useful to consider how we might observe a person who is struggling with any of these personal factors, and how we might help them through their challenges to get them back onto a more motivated track. The following are a few ideas worth consideration:

Leadership Actions That Impact Individual Sources of Demotivation

1. Interact frequently with each of your employees.
2. Consider matching employee personality and disposition in hiring and staffing decisions.
3. Include personality testing as part of employee development process.
4. Invest in employee development training to help employees build competence.
5. When "stretching" employees outside of their comfort zones, use frequent coaching and feedback to prevent motivational slumping.
6. Clarify expectations and assumptions directly with employees to avoid misunderstandings.
7. Pay attention to body language to assess motivational changes in employees.
8. Talk directly with employees about their motivation, rather than talking about them.

Interact frequently with each of your employees. As a manager, it's important that you get to know your employees; this includes understanding who they are, what drives them and how you might support them in their work. One approach is management by walking around. This means you get out of your office and walk around to listen and learn. Stop by to visit your employees in their workspace. Check on them and see how they're doing. Create an open dialogue to "check the pulse" of your department. Checking the pulse of an employee can be as simple as passing their desk and asking how they are doing. When someone who is normally chipper and happy to talk barely mumbles a hello, this is a sign that something isn't going well for them. These informal discussions can be insightful for the leader and can open the door to valuable conversations with employees when they are in the beginning stages of demotivation.

Consider matching employee personality and disposition in hiring and staffing decisions. Many of the challenges that lead to demotivation come from a mismatch between an individual's personality or disposition and the work that is required on the job. It is common for people to answer questions in an interview in ways that present themselves in the best possible light for the job that they are applying for, even if that is a mismatch with their true personalities and approaches to work. Hiring managers who are eager to fill open positions may not spend enough time or energy examining these personality and dispositional factors, which may add some additional steps in the hiring process or may be hard to assess. It is important to gather information about these individual differences as early as possible in order to avoid the issues that lead to demotivation once the person is hired.

Include personality assessments as part of the professional development and training process for employees. Doing so can help the organization to better understand employee preferences and then use that insight to support their career goals and aspirations. There are several instruments available such as DiSC and MBTI, and while we're not recommending that you adopt a particular instrument, we do recommend that you conduct research and determine if there's an option available that suits your organizational and employee needs. Doing so could help you to better position your employees by aligning their personality preferences with professional opportunities. For any of these instruments to work, a follow-up conversation with employees is critical. This gives everyone a better understanding of one another, which leads to improved interactions.

Invest in employee development training to help employees build competence. Provide a robust onboarding process where employees have the opportunity to acclimate to the organization in order to understand the formal processes and procedures, along with the informal "rules of the game." This initial investment of time and resources helps employees develop their competence, which in turn helps to build their confidence and sense of worth to the organization. As part of developing a learning organization, we recommend that you provide ongoing professional development and training opportunities for all employees. You can support this initiative by integrating it into the annual goal-setting process as part of your performance management system. For example, encourage employees to identify two or three goals that they will work toward during the year in support of strategic organizational priorities along with a professional development or training priority.

When "stretching" employees outside of their comfort zone, use frequent coaching and feedback to prevent motivational slumping. As employees are working through their development goals, it is really important to sit down with them to identify how you can support their goal attainment and developmental needs. Most people struggle as they begin to work on new skills, and that is when they most need leaders to engage them and provide additional support and encouragement. We would recommend that you meet at least quarterly with your employees to discuss how they're tracking toward their development goals. Of course, more frequent interactions may be needed if an employee is not progressing as intended or has requested the additional coaching and feedback.

Clarify expectations and assumptions directly with employees to avoid misunderstandings. One of the most important things that employees need from their leaders is a clear understanding of our expectations. It seems like it takes a lot of time and effort for leaders to constantly be checking in and clarifying, but it is actually more efficient to talk through expectations up front than to wait to clear up missed expectations after the employee starts working on a task. We know that managers are busy, and so we're not suggesting that you create new processes. Instead, look to integrate what we're recommending as part of what you're already doing. For example, based upon our professional experiences and best practices, managers should have an initial one-on-one meeting with the employee as part of the onboarding process and then continue those interactions at regularly scheduled intervals, such as quarterly, in order to provide the opportunity to clarify and address concerns.

Pay attention to body language to assess motivational changes in employees. While it is always important to maintain an open dialogue and rely on people to communicate their needs verbally, it is often our body language that demonstrates our needs, sometimes even before we realize that we have them. When we become frustrated or demotivated, we communicate with our facial expressions, posture, speed of movement, among other changes in our body language. If a leader is paying attention to these cues and notices a shift toward demotivated body language, it can provide a great opening for the leader to reach out and have a conversation with the employee. This "early intervention" is likely to help remove the motivational slump quickly, but is also likely to have the long-term impact of telling the employee that you care and you are willing to help them sort through their challenges.

Talk directly with employees about their motivation, rather than talking about them. When you invest in a relationship that has the purpose of making an employee feel valued, they will respond with the highest level of motivation. However, if they learn that you are talking about them, it erases all of the investments that you have made, damaging the trust that they believed existed between you, and causing them to question the validity of the relationship that they had built with you. If you have a concern about an employee's performance, it is really important that you talk to the employee directly, providing them with the level of meaningful feedback and coaching that maintains their sense of value as an employee.

Think You're Too Busy to Check in with Each Employee? *Think Again.*

When we talk to managers about checking the pulse of their workforce, many of them say that they "don't have time" to swing by and check the pulse of the seventy-four people who work in their department. So instead of checking in with some of their staff, they choose to check in with none of them. Having a ten-minute conversation with seventy-four employees every day would be a huge task; however, checking in doesn't require a huge effort. If you make checking in with a few different employees part of your daily routine, you will pick up on the pulse of your team. You don't have to touch everybody's life every single day in order to touch people's lives. One of the main reasons employees say they're happy in their workplaces is that they feel like their bosses care about them. You don't have to do much to show someone you care. A little attention can go a long way.

Now that you have reflected on the ideas provided, consider one person that you work with who may be struggling with motivation for any of the reasons that we have provided. In the reflection box provided, jot down ideas that you have for how you might be able to help that person. Understanding an individual's personality may be very useful in recognizing the risk of demotivation, and hopefully preventing their motivation from dropping.

REFLECTION:

Think of someone in your workplace who is demotivated, and consider which of the individual difference factors might be contributing to their demotivation. Write down two action ideas from the list on page 50 that you could use to address this situation.

_____

_____

_____

_____

_____

_____

FIVE SOURCES OF EMPLOYEE DEMOTIVATION

- Individual Differences
- Stressful Work
- Organizational Culture
- Conflict Between Co-Workers
- Leadership Style

Chapter 4:

WORKPLACE STRESS: HOW MUCH CAN ANY ONE PERSON TAKE?

As a regional marketing director for a major textbook publishing company, Sandra was responsible for supervising reps in multiple locations across the country. Sandra had a doctoral degree and a vast set of experiences within the publishing industry. When starting her job, she was eager to learn and to help the team. It was a high-pressure role because of the need to achieve sales goals, but Sandra was excited about the new opportunity and challenge.

The position was a promotion from her previous job and allowed her to use her professional skills and education. During initial staff meetings, it was clear that she was highly motivated, committed to her staff, and invested in the new career opportunity. She reported to James, an executive vice president. James had been with the publishing company for several years and had been successful in a variety of institutional roles. He delivered results and sought to get the best from his people. James was also known as a bully who wasn't afraid to belittle and threaten others to achieve the desired outcomes. Sandra's working relationship with James started out well, but over time, the relationship soured as he blamed Sandra for the team's failure to achieve sales goals. James didn't seem to recognize that Sandra didn't have the resources needed to achieve the goals because of rep vacancies and a lack of support from the company in terms of poorly designed marketing campaigns and lack of funding for promotional events. The lack of resources and support led to grueling twelve-hour workdays and working weekends.

After six months it became evident, in subtle ways, that Sandra was overwhelmed and had lost her internal motivation as a result of on-the-job stressors. She became less engaged during meetings, making few contributions. She began missing meetings and was unavailable for events. She began spending less time with the team. She was stressed and demotivated. To compound matters, she also began experiencing health consequences, such as sleeplessness, migraines, and weight loss. In fact, she lost so much weight that one of her coworkers who hadn't seen her for a month was shocked by her physical change. So, one Monday evening, without notice, Sandra sent a text message to her team notifying them that she was resigning, effective immediately, because of the pressures of the job. It was literally making her sick.

Before we move on to the rest of the chapter, we want to remind you that, of the five sources of demotivation, employees are only responsible for one: individual differences, which we discussed in Chapter 3. Most of the time when we see a demotivated employee, we only think of individual differences. This is referred to as the fundamental attribution error, a tendency to overestimate the impact of an individual's personality and underestimate the impact of the situation or environment when explaining the cause of behavior. We think that their personality is flawed, that they are lazy, or that they're carrying baggage. We pay no attention to the things that we might be doing as managers and leaders to demotivate them. It's easier to write off demotivated employees as lazy than it is to see how we might be demotivating them. For the rest of this book, we will be addressing the sources of demotivation that managers and leaders can control.

SHORT-TERM VERSUS LONG-TERM STRESS

Not long after Sandra quit her job, her husband approached her and told her that he felt she had completely changed; that after quitting her job, she had returned to the woman he had fallen in love with. She was no longer snapping at the family, constantly on edge, or restless in her sleep. Sandra was surprised by his comment. She hadn't realized how much the stress had been affecting her life or her family. The stress she thought she had been taking on short-term had actually turned into a chronic condition.

If Sandra had experienced short-term stress due to a single project that had lasted a week or so, her motivation basket might have suffered a small hole. But since she experienced long-term stress—her workspace was stressful for six months—a giant hole ripped through her motivation basket. Therefore, an employee who had been highly motivated had quickly turned into one who couldn't stand to continue working in her existing environment.

WHEN YOU THINK ABOUT SHORT-TERM VERSUS LONG-TERM STRESS, THINK ABOUT THE DIFFERENCE BETWEEN SPRINTING AND LONG-DISTANCE RUNNING. IMAGINE TRYING TO KEEP A SPRINTER'S PACE THROUGHOUT AN ENTIRE MARATHON.

If an employee receives a call from a customer who wants to increase the volume of their order with a short turnaround time, that's a good problem to have. It might temporarily feel stressful, but once the employee solves it, they get to feel the exhilaration of accomplishing a job. That feeling can positively motivate someone. It can activate them and get them going. But no one can do that long-term. When you think about short-term versus long-term stress, think about the difference between sprinting and long-distance running. Imagine trying to keep a sprinter's pace throughout an entire marathon. That would be impossible, as Sandra's experience proves.

The title of this chapter, "Workplace Stress: How Much Can Any One Person Take?" discusses the lived experiences, like Sandra's, and the research regarding stress in the workplace. It's important to consider job stress and its relationship to employee motivation, because there are implications for understanding how stress causes employees to lose their motivation and to become demotivated. Several research studies have concluded that there's an inverse relationship between job stress and employee motivation. If stress levels are up, employee motivation is down.

WHAT IS WORKPLACE STRESS?

Simply defined, workplace stress is the pressure we feel to perform at some predetermined level as measured by a result or outcome. Selye has described it as a "dynamic condition in which an individual is confronted with an opportunity, constraint or demand, related to what he or she desires and for which the outcome is perceived to be both uncertain and important" (Selye 1979). The National Institute for Occupational Safety and Health (NIOSH) states "job stress refers to the harmful physical and emotional responses that occur when the requirements of the job do not match the capabilities, resources, or needs of the worker." In order to create the best possible conditions for human workers to perform well, it is important to understand how stress tolerance levels, motivating mechanisms, support needs and the desire to have influence over the workplace impact a worker. The relationship between our emotional well-being, our mental health, our personal welfare, and our social environment is important. In a workplace context, it's essential to understand that there's a relationship between our environment and how we feel about ourselves. How stressed we are directly impacts how mentally healthy we are. Understanding this is important because one of the main environments we all spend time in is our work environment. This ability to recognize the factors that facilitate a healthy work environment are consequential because of the implications for employee turnover, engagement and job satisfaction.

Moreover, in understanding what constitutes a healthy work environment, we must acknowledge that while stress has a negative connotation, it is not always a bad thing. While prolonged stress like the stress Sandra experienced can be harmful to our physical well-being and mental health, short periods of stress can actually be helpful, as stress causes us to work efficiently under pressure to achieve goals or to summon our "cave man" instincts to address sudden dangers or threats as part of our instinctive "fight or flight" response mechanism.

While short periods of stress can be beneficial, chronic stress is a health hazard. When people are stressed at work, they experience an increase in their blood pressure, which has certain cardiovascular effects including an increase in type 2 diabetes onset. When people are stressed, they don't eat as well or exercise as much as they should because they end up dealing with work instead of taking care of themselves. Work-related stress often forces a person to spend more time prioritizing work above anything else. The tradeoff for workplace stress is letting go of healthy habits like exercise and nutrition.

You might be asking yourself, Why is this important? Why should I care? Those are fair questions, so we've identified two reasons you should care.

- In its 2017 *Mind the Workplace Report* (Hellebuyck et al. 2017), Mental Health America (MHA) cited the 2016 research of Harvard researcher Joel Goh and Stanford researchers Jeffrey Pfeffer and Stefanos Zenios (Goh et al. 2016). They performed a meta-analysis of 228 studies in order to assess the effect of ten common workplace stressors on health. The study found that as many as 120,000 deaths every year may be attributable to stress in the workplace. "When we consider that these are premature deaths, this is a number one killer."

- Returning to the 2017 Gallup poll on employee engagement, findings indicate that workplace stress is an important contributor to low levels of employee engagement. It's estimated that disengaged workers cost as much as $500 billion annually in lost productivity.

A highly competitive business environment driven by key metrics such as sales and profit goals, tight budgets, and even timelines can overwhelm employees. It's not surprising that more than 70 percent of respondents to the Workplace Health Survey, as reported in *Mind the Workplace*, felt their firms had unrealistic workload expectations, and a majority of survey respondents reported a lack of support across all ranks in their workplace (Hellebuyck et al. 2017). More bad news continued with only 36 percent reporting they could rely on their supervisors and 34 percent on their colleagues. Given that support from supervisors and coworkers was strongly correlated with overall job satisfaction, we can see how this stressor is contributing to workplace demotivation.

The Workplace Health Survey also measured workplace stress and specifically focused on the role a negative work environment had on employees' abilities to perform their jobs, maintain their relationships, and preserve their mental health. We know from previous research findings that stress at work contributes to higher levels of absenteeism, and the results were similar in this survey. Of the respondents, 33 percent responded they "always, often, or sometimes" missed work due to stress. Of those who "always or often" missed work due to the stress, 53 percent missed six or more days each month. That's at least seventy-two days per year! Even more striking is that even when workplace stress didn't result in absenteeism, it still significantly affected employee engagement. This is consequential because as previously noted in the Gallup (2017) study, lost productivity can result in losses approaching half a billion dollars. Results from the Workplace Health Survey suggest "workplace stress is mitigated by leadership that promotes strong positive work ethics, including a sense of teamwork and responsibility." Findings also suggest that leadership can promote fair and reliable workplace practices in order to increase employee engagement and help to reduce feelings of isolation and negative attitudes toward the workplace. We know from our professional experiences that workplace stress has real consequences, and Sandra's story reminds us of the ramifications.

While employees have a responsibility to manage their job stress, there are definitive actions that leaders can take in order to reduce the stress levels of employees.

Leadership Actions to Reduce the Demotivating Effect of Workplace Stress

1. Engage employees from the beginning of a potentially stressful situation.
2. Acknowledge the stress impact (rather than pretending it doesn't exist).
3. Monitor the demand levels of the work, especially for high-performing employees.
4. Provide frequent opportunities for employees to engage in stress-relieving activities.
5. Step up and pitch in to complete tasks that add stress to employees.
6. Remove obstacles that may increase stress for employees.
7. Increase predictability in processes and communication patterns to help employees achieve a sense of control over their stress.
8. Celebrate successes of effort, attitude, and endurance during stressful times.

Engage employees from the beginning of a potentially stressful situation. Although some stressful events are difficult to anticipate, it is rather common for leaders to know about major changes or activities that will add stress to the work of their employees. The hardest part for employees who are dealing with these stressors is the lack of control or time to prepare for the changes that they are facing. When a manager engages employees early in the planning stages for the stressful event, they are demonstrating a concern for the employee and valuing the input that the employee might have in implementing the changes associated with the stressful event. This gives the employee more time to prepare, as well as a greater sense of control over the process, because their input is valued by their leaders.

Acknowledge the stress impact (rather than pretending it doesn't exist). Because stress is very common in the workplace, we can become jaded about the impact of stress on employees. As leaders, we may become dismissive of the negative reactions that employees express when we present them with stressful situations. When people identify the stress that they are experiencing, we need to resist the urge to respond with sayings such as "that's what we pay you the big bucks for" or "suck it up, buttercup." Usually a bit of empathy goes a long way toward showing your employees that you understand the stress they are experiencing, and the support from your acknowledgment may prevent their motivation from hitting rock bottom.

Rather than waiting for employees to come to you with their complaints about stress, you can initiate the conversation. It is not difficult to guess when an employee is likely to be feeling stressed out, so reaching out gives them a chance to vent. Your support can be very welcome, and may help them to put a temporary patch on the holes in their baskets of motivation.

Monitor the demand levels of the work, especially for high-performing employees. One of the most common complaints that we hear from high-performing employees is that they feel they are being punished for top performance, because they get even more work to do than the average coworker. Nothing is worse for a leader than to have their highest performers feeling the effects of stress and demotivation. Not only does it impact the productivity and quality of the high-performing employee, but the rest of the team will follow suit if they recognize that the top performer is demotivated. Also, as part of monitoring demand levels, look for opportunities to offer flexible work arrangements/workday flexibility, which will provide employees with the chance to have more autonomy and control over how they manage the increased work demands.

Provide frequent opportunities for employees to engage in stress-relieving activities. This may include relaxation exercises, cognitive behavioral interventions (such as techniques for replacing pessimism with more optimistic or realistic thinking), meditation, or various forms of play that allow employees to take a break from the stressful situations that they encounter. It is amazing how a short break changes your perspective and your energy, especially when you are dealing with a stressful situation.

> IT MAY BE THAT THE LEADER HOLDS QUICK UPDATE MEETINGS WITH INDIVIDUALS OR WITH THE TEAM OR PROVIDES SOME SORT OF ELECTRONIC UPDATES THAT ARE CONSISTENT AND PREDICTABLE, SO THAT EMPLOYEES GET THE INFORMATION THEY NEED DURING STRESSFUL TIMES.

Step up and pitch in to complete tasks that add stress to employees. When leaders pitch in to help employees during heavy work periods, they send some very important signals to the team. The leader who works alongside employees is showing them respect and demonstrating genuine concern for the challenges that they are facing. If the leader offers up an "extra pair of hands" they are acting as a member of the team, joining in the camaraderie, and increasing their understanding of the individuals who work under them.

Remove obstacles that may increase stress for employees.

Sometimes the stress that an employee faces is related to their organizational power, or lack thereof, which may present obstacles that they struggle to overcome. In other instances the obstacles are related to a lack of resources such as financial support or cooperation from another department. If the leader is able to understand and take actions to help remove obstacles, an employee can quickly recover from any issues of demotivation that they may have been experiencing from that source of stress.

Increase predictability in processes and communication patterns to help employees achieve a sense of control over their stress. During times of stress, people need information. They especially need to know how the changes in the stressful event will impact them personally. This drive to understand and predict future outcomes is very important for leaders to recognize and address. When employees do not get the information that they need, they turn to the grapevine, which fills the void with assumptions and rumors. It may be that the leader holds quick update meetings with individuals or with the team or provides some sort of electronic updates that are consistent and predictable, so that employees get the information that they need during stressful times.

Celebrate successes of effort, attitude, and endurance during stressful times. Everyone loves a celebration, even if it is a quick and symbolic gesture that recognizes the completion of a major milestone. This is especially true when completing a stressful event, whether at the individual or team level. Make sure to take the time to recognize the effort and bring some closure to the stressful event, which will likely help people rebound to their former motivational state more quickly.

While these eight actions aren't necessarily a panacea in terms of "curing" or removing the source of the stress, leaders can help employees reduce stress levels and the "sinking feeling" that comes with demotivation.

REFLECTION:

Consider a current or recent situation in your workplace in which employees are feeling additional stress in completing their jobs. Choose two of the eight leadership actions discussed in this chapter that you believe would help your employees. Write them down and then list how you might put them into action.

_____

_____

_____

_____

_____

_____

FIVE SOURCES OF EMPLOYEE DEMOTIVATION

- Individual Differences
- Stressful Work
- Organizational Culture
- Conflict Between Co-Workers
- Leadership Style

Chapter 5:

ORGANIZATIONAL CULTURE: WHO CAN STAY MOTIVATED IN A PLACE LIKE THIS?

Last winter, Tara was on her way from Houston to Chicago. Not long after she got to the Houston airport, she got one of those dreaded texts from the airline about a flight delay that had no estimated departure time. Anyone who flies to the Midwest or the East Coast in the winter knows to expect delays due to unpredictable weather. So, even though it was sunny in Houston, Tara walked to the gate with the expectation that she might be grounded for a while. She sat down, opened her laptop and started catching up on email while she waited for the weather to clear.

As time ticked on with little news from the airline, the mass of people waiting at Gate D37 started to get antsy and then angry. One by one, customers started swarming the customer service desk looking for answers. Would they miss their connection in Chicago? Could they be rerouted through another city? Would vouchers be given if the delay lasted any longer? Always interested in how large companies handle crisis situations, Tara perked up and watched and listened as the tension grew.

The first thing Tara noticed was that every single one of the six gate agents refused to make eye contact with the passengers, let alone answer their questions. Finally, after nonstop pestering from customers, the agents started responding, but their responses were curt and unhelpful. Of course no one expects gate agents to know when weather will clear, but they do expect them to at least politely answer questions about what might happen if the flight delay continues.

In addition to avoiding customers, the gate agents would occasionally whisper to the flight attendants in front of the customers. No one could hear what they were saying, but it was clear that some information or speculation was being withheld. To make matters worse, the agents and flight attendants would occasionally roll their eyes. This type of communication makes customers feel invisible, disrespected, and uneasy. What is going on and why aren't they allowed to know anything about what's happening?

Nearly two hours after the departure time, the passengers were allowed to board the plane. No explanation or apology was given regarding the delay, and when the gate agents took the tickets, they did so aggressively and without making eye contact. When asked about the delay, they said something along the lines of "It's the weather. We can't do anything about the weather. We know you're frustrated, but we are frustrated, too." The attitude expressed with the explanation was one of hostility and irritation rather than compassion and understanding.

Between boarding and takeoff, there was no explanation or apology from the pilot or the flight staff. Tara was shocked to hear the flight attendants go into their safety speech and then prepare for takeoff without saying a word to the customers about the delay or their plans for making up for it. When the plane landed, no one thanked the passengers or invited them to enjoy the rest of their day. To add insult to injury, Tara's bags never arrived. While lost bags are a hazard of air travel, the staff at the reclaim counter treated Tara as rudely as the staff in Houston had treated the customers who wanted to know what was happening with their flights. From a customer support standpoint, the experience that Tara and the other passengers had on that flight from Houston to Chicago was absolutely inexcusable. As a person who is interested in demotivation, the experience was a great one for Tara, who later used it to show her students what happens when the culture of an organization blasts holes in the motivation baskets of each of its employees.

Have you ever found yourself in a situation like Tara's? Have you ever experienced an organization in which it was clear to you that most of the employees hated their jobs? The signs of this dissatisfaction are overwhelming, especially if you are the customer, and it becomes very challenging to do business with folks who are so clearly demotivated. No matter how hard you try as a customer, you cannot find anyone to smile at you. They are quick to tell you why they cannot solve your problem or change their procedures, implying that it is not their fault. They move slowly through their tasks, and they appear to wish they were anywhere but at that job at that time. You start by thinking that the person you are working with is a "dud" of some sort, but then you look around and see that this is basically how all of the employees seem to be acting, and you suddenly also wish you were anywhere but there. Unfortunately we both have experienced many organizations that appear to have this culture that produces demotivated workers.

Contrast that with organizational cultures that create exciting and dynamic places to work, where people seem genuinely proud of their jobs and their company, and the positive energy is contagious. Although we started this chapter explaining a negative workplace culture and how that negativity can impact employee motivation, there are plenty of examples of companies that know how to keep their employees motivated. Cathy recently traveled from Miami to Detroit and experienced a flight delay exactly as Tara did. However, Cathy's experience was completely different. As soon as Cathy got to the gate, a friendly airline staff member rolled a tray of cookies, water, and coffee through the waiting area. Then one of the staff members got on the speaker and said, "Hey folks, this is frustrating. Come up and get a complimentary snack." As the delay continued, the airline staff gave frequent updates, answered customer questions with a smile, and did everything within their power to make the experience less miserable. When the plane finally boarded, the flight attendants profusely apologized for the delay and the captain made a very personal announcement, first thanking everyone for flying with the airline and then apologizing for the delay and explaining what had caused it.

> NO MATTER HOW MUCH MOTIVATION YOU HAVE WHEN YOU ENTER YOUR WORKPLACE, THE CULTURE AROUND YOU IS A MAJOR FACTOR IN FEEDING (OR STARVING) YOUR MOTIVATION...

Companies such as the airline that Cathy flew on, Google, St. Jude's Hospital, Publix Supermarkets, Boston Consulting Group, Hilton, and many others have been described by employees as "great places to work," based on criteria such as employee engagement, pride, and sense of community. No matter how much motivation you have when you enter your workplace, the culture around you is a major factor in feeding (or starving) your motivation, which is why we chose to examine this as the primary demotivating source in this chapter.

In fact, you may recall Cathy's experience on the Hawaiian Islands cruise in Chapter 3 where employees also hated their jobs. In that situation, the source of demotivation was individual differences.

In this chapter, the source of demotivation is the organizational culture. Noting this point of distinction is important. You'll need to take the time to really understand the source of the demotivation so that you don't misattribute it.

The study of organizational culture has been the focus of several researchers over the past few decades. The definition is best described by businessdictionary.com as follows: "The values and behaviors that contribute to the unique social and psychological environment of an organization." Organizational culture includes an organization's expectations, experiences, and philosophy, and the values that hold it together. It is expressed in its self-image, inner workings, interactions with the outside world, and future expectations. It is based on shared attitudes, beliefs, customs, and written and unwritten rules that have been developed over time and are considered valid. Also called corporate culture, it's shown in:

- The ways the organization conducts its business and treats its employees, customers, and the wider community.
- The extent to which freedom is allowed in decision-making, developing new ideas, and personal expression.
- How power and information flow through its hierarchy.
- How committed employees are toward organizational goals.

Edgar Schein (2016) provides an overview of what comprises an organizational culture in which he identifies three categories that provide evidence of the culture of an organization. The first includes the artifacts that show evidence of culture, such as the dress code or office furniture. The second category is shared values on the issues and goals that matter to people in the organization. Finally, the third category is what he calls assumed values, which refers to beliefs and facts that are hidden but relevant to the culture of the organization, such as unwritten rules of communication and conduct that are well-known but not discussed.

Some scholars have chosen to describe culture by identifying different types of culture and indicating the extent to which these types of culture are a good fit for the goals and people who work within an organization. It is worth noting that organizations are likely to have one formal type of culture while also having subcultures that exist informally or within specific departments of an organization. In the research conducted by Kim Cameron and Robert Quinn (2011), there are four types of organizational cultures that exist in most workplaces. These are clan, adhocracy, hierarchal, and market cultures. The box on the following page breaks down each of these cultures by their defining characteristics.

FOUR CATEGORIES OF ORGANIZATIONAL CULTURE

Based on the Competing Values Framework

CLAN

- Empowerment
- Team Building
- Employee Involvement
- Employee Development
- Open Communication

ADHOCRACY

- Surprise and Delight
- Creating New Standards
- Anticipating Needs
- Continuous Improvement
- Finding Creative Solutions

HIERARCHY

- Error Detection
- Measurement
- Process Control
- Systematic Problem-Solving
- Quality Tools

MARKET

- Measuring Customer Preferences
- Improving Productivity
- Creating External Partnerships
- Enhancing Competitiveness
- Involving Customers and Suppliers

Source: Cameron and Quinn 2011

Each of these four categories makes sense in certain situations and industries but may also be difficult for some people to adjust to, which may lead to their demotivation at work. Let's take a look at each of these cultures and see how they might impact both motivation and demotivation.

CLAN CULTURE

One of the most famous examples of a clan culture is online shoe and clothing retailer Zappos. Zappos has a tight-knit culture. They offer various benefits to their employees; allow for flex-time, job sharing, and telecommuting; and provide onsite daycare as well as an onsite fitness center to help people balance their work and family lives. The Zappos culture is more of a supportive family culture than anything else. When a person works for Zappos, they are a part of that clan. Zappos is not the kind of organization in which individuals are trying to meet their quota and beat other people down the hall. It's a very communal, supportive culture. Zappos CEO Tony Hsieh talks about building a positive team and a family spirit, but his commitment to this isn't just lip service. It really is embedded in the organization. This is why in clan cultures people tend to feel loyal to the organization: they know the organization cares about them, so they care right back. Employees who work in a clan culture feel like their managers and coworkers care about them. Each of the things that happen in the clan culture has as its purpose that sense of building community, family, bonds, and loyalty.

The characteristics of a clan culture, which include empowerment, team building, employee involvement, employee development, and open communication, make employees understand that they're going to be heard. As a result, they are more engaged and less likely to leave. Clan cultures focus on investing in the growth and development of their employees. This creates a feeling of trust and empowerment among employees who feel like they're part of the decision-making process. When people feel valued, they are more likely to raise their hands to do something and therefore more likely to be engaged in the community of the organization.

Anyone can become demotivated in any culture, but one of the advantages of a clan culture is that because it's so supportive, when someone feels demotivated—when those holes start appearing in their motivation basket—there are plenty of other people around them to help fill the holes. That support makes people feel less alone.

People who like teamwork and collaboration, and who are motivated by the energy of working with others, are likely to love working in a clan culture. That being said, because clan cultures are so inclusive, some people may not feel like they fit in. They may see everyone else fitting in just fine, and that may make them feel like an outsider. Those who feel "left out of the clan" will be demotivated rather quickly in this specific culture. This is not very common, which is why clan cultures also seem to have a lot fewer issues with employee demotivation than other cultures we will examine.

ADHOCRACY CULTURE

An adhocracy culture is characterized by innovation and creativity. Google and Apple are two large companies that work within the adhocracy model.

In adhocracies, you see a lot of what you might refer to as nonconforming behavior. In these cultures, you won't see evidence of formalities like dress codes or prescribed work hours, but you will see a lot more flexibility. As noted previously, Google has been recognized on several occasions as one of the best places to work. This is reflected in the flexibility provided to employees in terms of work schedules. Moreover, Google has been known for its "Twenty Percent Time," a policy which encourages employees to spend one day per week on a pet project. This type of structure can be very motivating because it provides a level of autonomy and control that appeals to employees who value this type of culture.

In an adhocracy, teamwork is temporary in nature. It's designed around short-burst idea generation. Adhocracy culture feeds off the excitement of coming up with a new invention, which is why this culture is likely a very good match for people attracted to creativity and problem-solving. Creativity and problem-solving through the use of teams is an inherent way of doing business at Apple and is part of the company's DNA. Design and engineering teams have worked together to come up with innovations like the "Speaktenna" (combination of speakers and antennas for Wi-Fi and Bluetooth in the MacBook) that had never been tried previously. This type of breakthrough isn't likely to happen without teamwork. This is something that Apple understands very well, and so the company utilizes teamwork and collaboration to support its culture of innovation. Because employees are engaged in activities that fill their motivation baskets, they're likely more engaged and committed to the firm.

Companies that work within this model often keep scoreboards that celebrate people who did something well. In an adhocracy, people also tend to be motivated by the contributions that they make. Those who tend to be demotivated by an adhocracy culture usually need more structure in the workplace. These people need formal mechanisms for feedback and promotions. If you're a person who needs predictability, it's going to be hard to have that in an adhocracy culture. It is exciting to join a dynamic company such as Google or Apple, but if this is not a good fit with how you like to work, you may be surprised to find demotivation creeping in.

HIERARCHY CULTURE

The most common culture that people describe as demotivating is the hierarchy culture, which tends to be characterized by a lot of rules and procedures, a chain of command for decision-making and other communications, and a clear path for career progression. The military, institutions of higher education, and manufacturing facilities typically have a hierarchy culture.

Organizations with a hierarchy structure are either set up under leadership philosophies that have been around for more than a hundred years, or they're set up to support the nature of the work being done. For example, the military has to have a hierarchy culture because if a chain of command is not followed, people can die. There's a safety issue there. The same goes for most manufacturing jobs in which safety is a factor. If processes are not followed in a manufacturing environment, someone may suffer an injury. Organizations that have a lot of processes and external rules to follow will also likely adopt a hierarchy culture. For example, in higher education, there are processes for everything. If a part-time faculty member needs to be hired, for example, the approval for the hire may need to go through three or four people, making a decision that could take anywhere between a day and several weeks. One of the issues with this type of organizational structure is that with so many processes in place, it doesn't allow individuals to make decisions for themselves, and decision-making can get bogged down by the formal process.

While a hierarchy culture may make sense in controlling for errors that could exist in systems and processes, it takes a toll on the motivation of individuals, who may not feel like there is an avenue for their ideas or for creative problem-solving. This is especially true for highly skilled employees as well as knowledge workers, who likely chose their profession because it matched with the investment that they made in developing a specific expertise, only to find that the company preferred that they keep their ideas to themselves and simply follow protocols. There's so much structure that people can't make simple choices for themselves, and going through the hierarchical approval process can really become a bottleneck. The chain-of-command process for communication can also have a strongly negative impact on motivation, as people may not find their needs met in a timely manner, and they may not believe that they are highly valued by the managers in their organization.

There are many positive motivational aspects of this culture for some people. If you go into a Bank of America, you want to have a comparable experience whether you're in Denver or Seattle. Standardization in large organizations helps to do that. People who like having systems and clearly defined procedures in place might embrace working for a hierarchy culture. Additionally, rules and structure can help improve efficiency of operations, reduce error in communications, and prevent the company from experiencing the legal ramifications associated with violating laws. Given the range of reasons why some organizations adopt a hierarchy culture, it is important for leaders and managers to pay close attention to the high risk for demotivating employees with the rules, structures and processes that are in place.

MARKET CULTURE

Likewise, the market culture is a great match for the highly extro-verted person who is motivated by interaction with customers and partners along the supply chain, as well as people who love the challenge of meeting and exceeding customer needs.

Quicken Loans is a great example of a company with a market culture. Quicken Loans is an innovative company, but that innovation centers around understanding how a customer wants to go through the mortgage process and then reinventing the way that process is completed. Internally, competition is high. Those who work at Quicken Loans are high-energy. They have a high level of opportunity and lots of customer training, and they put a lot of energy into understanding customers and their values.

Some people feed off working in a competitive environment. They like looking at a scorecard and seeing themselves doing well. They also like having their income tied to performance. But in an environment where there is a lot of winning, there are also people who are not winning. For the individuals who are not winning, a market culture can be very demotivating. Burnout can be an issue. It can lead to health issues stemming from long-term stress, which we talked about in Chapter 4.

Highly motivated people who work in a market culture can also become demotivated, particularly if the systems for compensation and rewards, as well as opportunities for advancement, focus too much on productivity. It is common for managers to build in production goals and incentives that may actually inhibit problem-solving, teamwork, creativity, or networking, by causing employees to focus on production activities that are different from the activities that motivate them. Some will be successful in meeting the production goals, and the rewards may replace their lack of job satisfaction, but this tends to be only a temporary patch to the drain on their motivation.

Now that we've explained the four typical organizational cultures, read through this example and see if you can identify which type of culture Angela is working in and how that culture has impacted her motivation.

Angela loved her job at a regional marketing company in the Pacific Northwest. She was a member of a creative team of eleven people and really enjoyed her relationships with her coworkers and boss and the folks in other departments. She was an expert in her field, and she felt empowered and challenged every day, which made her proud of the company that she worked for and the work that she produced there. She kept unusual hours, because she was a single mom who had to juggle the responsibilities of caring for her young child. It was common for her to work from home well into the late hours of the night, and she also worked on the weekends when something inspired her or she was facing a deadline. Many of Angela's coworkers maintained unique schedules for a variety of reasons, and they adopted a number of ways to stay in communication even when they were not all at work together. Angela estimated that she put in somewhere around sixty hours of work per week, but she didn't mind, because she loved the work and got to do it on her own time.

As is common in the industry, Angela's company was sold to a larger marketing firm with offices located in major cities around the world and headquarters in New York. At first, Angela and her colleagues were thrilled about the potential opportunities of this large company, but that didn't last very long. As they transitioned to the new company, they had a number of meetings and memos that provided them with the policies and procedures. Many of the tools and processes they used were being replaced by new ones from "Big Brother" (as Angela and her colleagues referred to their new company). All of the communications with people from "Big Brother" were one-way, and nobody really ever asked Angela or her colleagues for input or ideas. The new policy that struck the biggest blow was the system for tracking hours (so that clients could be billed for their work). This system required Angela and the others to clock in and out, and this could only be done on the equipment at the office. This removed any possibility of doing work at home. A related issue was the amount of attention that "Big Brother" managers paid to the number of hours worked and the time of day they started and ended, which seemed to be much more important to them than the quality of the work. Angela rearranged her life so that she could clock in at 8 a.m. and leave exactly at 5 p.m. every day, and she avoided doing any additional work from home. Every week, another member of the team left the company for a new job, until only a few were left, feeling as though they were chained to their desks. Angela lasted eight months and then took her expertise, her work ethic, and her passion to another company.

As you read through the example of the new "Big Brother" company that acquired Angela's firm, did you recognize that this is likely a hierarchy culture, which involved a primary focus on procedures and rules and "chain of command" decision-making? It is common for people to lose motivation in this type of organizational culture, so let's spend a few minutes considering ideas that might help your organization make changes to create a more motivating culture.

As you examine the different types of organizational culture and think about the example of Angela's two organizations, take a moment to reflect on the organization that you currently work in. Can you identify the culture that you believe describes your organization the best? Is this the right fit for you and your values and approach to work? How might it be a challenge for some of the folks that work with you? The impact on employee demotivation may be direct, in terms of a misfit between the organizational culture and an employee's values and preferred approach to work; for other employees, the fact that their own department has an organizational culture that is not aligned with the broad organization could be a cause for demotivation.

In examining the four cultures described, you can see that there are differences in how information flows through organizations. In some organizations, it flows freely, with frequent communication about values, processes, expectations, and changes. In some organizational cultures, employees feel welcome to participate in gathering and understanding the issues that impact their jobs. In other organizations, employees work with vague messages that leave quite a lot of ambiguity about the organization's values, mission, goals, strategies and processes. In these organizations, the employees tend to feel frustrated by the uncertainty and unpredictability of the environment they work in. This is the type of situation in which the rumor mill takes over and fills the ambiguous space with all sorts of negative energy and speculation. The lack of clear communication tends to breed distrust of management, and can be very demotivating to workers.

One area in which this problem is most critical is in the area of compensation practices. When these practices lack transparency, individuals become very skeptical of and frustrated with what they perceive to be a lack of procedural justice. This construct refers to an employee's sense of the fairness of the process by which a decision is made (Posthuma et al. 2007). It is important for these processes to be transparent so that employees understand how compensation and other HR decisions are made in general, and specifically for their own situation, or they are likely to feel like victims of a mysterious process that they do not control, which is highly demotivating.

So how can you make sure that the culture of your own organization has the most positive impact on employee motivation, and avoids some of the pitfalls that have been identified? Based on our experiences and the wisdom of many scholars, we offer you several ideas for actions that you can take as a leader to create a great organizational culture for your employees.

Leadership Actions to Prevent a Demotivating Organizational Culture

1. Assess the culture of your organization and the impact that the culture is having on employees.

2. Engage employees in understanding their expectations and preferences for organizational culture.

3. Engage other managers and leaders in the organization, as well as stakeholders such as customers or vendors, to understand how they view the culture of the organization as well as the subculture of your department.

4. Consider the impact of how information flows through your organization, and examine whether this matches the needs of employees.

5. Examine how your leadership style and expectations for employees in your department match (or differ from) the overall culture of the organization.

6. If your department requires a different culture than the organizational culture, make adjustments to build the culture that works best within the department.

7. Celebrate your organizational culture within your own department.

8. Dare to change your organizational culture if the one you have is demotivating your employees.

Assess the culture of your organization and the impact that the culture is having on employees. It is useful for all leaders to begin a process of evaluating your organization's culture and comparing that to the goals, mission, vision, and values of the organization. If you are in an executive-level position, make sure that you do not do this alone; rather, you should engage as many stakeholders as possible in determining the type of organizational culture that makes the most sense for success in the future. You might consider using the Organizational Culture Assessment Instrument (OCAI), which is based upon the four cultures discussed in this chapter.

Engage employees in understanding their expectations and preferences for organizational culture. Although the culture of an organization is likely established by the founders and tends to be stable over time, it is important to engage employees in discussing the culture of the organization and understanding where the culture creates challenges for them. This may be accomplished through formal mechanisms such as employee satisfaction surveys as well as informal conversations with employees.

Engage other managers and leaders in the organization, as well as stakeholders such as customers or vendors, to understand how they view the culture of the organization as well as the subculture of your department. Although people may not be able to describe the organizational culture formally, most people have a clear sense of what it is like to work with your organization, which is evidence of the culture. Consider checking with people in other departments, customers, vendors and other stakeholders to see how they view the culture and to understand any challenges that they encounter when working with it. Again, this can be done through the use of surveys as well as informal discussions.

Consider the impact of how information flows through your organization, and examine whether this matches the needs of employees. Take some time to understand the flow of information between you and the employees in your department, between the people in your department and others, and overall within the organization. The flow of information provides excellent evidence of the type of culture that your employees are experiencing. You might consider evaluating your current key business process maps to understand how information flows between departments. If those process maps don't exist, you could start by creating them in your department (start small and just pick one key process) and then engaging with other departments to establish a "current state" and then a "desired state" process map which addresses any gaps or concerns.

Examine how your leadership style and expectations for employees in your department match (or differ from) the overall culture of the organization. An interesting thing about organizational culture is that it doesn't only include the entire organization, but also the subcultures within it. These subcultures are created by a leader of a portion of the organization, and can be specific to a single department. There are multiple leadership style assessments available, so pick one and then compare the behaviors of the leadership style with the desired "behaviors" in your company's organizational culture. If there's a mismatch, identify ways to close the gap, such as implementing the recommendations provided by the assessment, hiring a coach, or getting feedback from your mentor.

If your department requires a different culture than the organizational culture, make adjustments to build the culture that works best within the department. If you are not at the executive level of your organization, you may find it more challenging, but you need to find a way to communicate your concerns and goals for improving the culture of the organization if you believe it is worthwhile to take on this challenge. For example, if your company utilizes an employee survey, this can be a "safe" way to share your concerns and ideas on how to improve. If you are a middle manager, you can also create your own subculture inside your part of the organization, and you can involve others to help you to create and implement the necessary changes.

> CELEBRATING YOUR CULTURE CAN COME IN MANY FORMS, AND MAY BE AS SIMPLE AS HAVING TEAM LOGOS ON T-SHIRTS, COFFEE MUGS, OR OTHER FORMS OF "SWAG" THAT ALLOW PEOPLE TO DISPLAY THEIR PRIDE.

Celebrate your organizational culture within your own department. It is important for people to appreciate and relate to the organization that they work for. As a leader, you can help establish norms that engender the feelings of pride and affective commitment that help remind people about the motivation that they have for their work. Celebrating your culture can come in many forms, and may be as simple as having team logos on T-shirts, coffee mugs, or other forms of "swag" that allow people to display their pride.

Dare to change your organizational culture if the one you have is demotivating your employees. Although it can be challenging to shift organizational culture, it is not impossible. As you pay closer attention to the impact of your organization's culture on the demotivation of your employees, you may want to engage others in changing your organizational culture. As you begin on a journey to a new organizational culture, you will find a lot of challenges along the way. As a leader in the organization, you must be very careful not to slip back into the behaviors of the old culture. Make sure to model the new behavior ("walk the talk"). People will need training and ongoing support as they try on the new behaviors, and it will need to be OK for them to struggle as they improve the processes and communication patterns of the new organizational culture. Along these lines, it will be very helpful to check in frequently with people all through the organization. Make sure to celebrate small wins as people adopt new approaches, to reinforce their effort in the new direction. None of these changes will work if you do not realign metrics and rewards with the new cultural behaviors that you are expecting.

REFLECTION:

Based on the descriptions provided, what do you believe is the type of organizational culture that you and your employees work within? From the leadership actions provided, write down two ideas that will help you ensure that the organizational culture doesn't poke holes in your employees' motivation baskets.

_____

_____

_____

_____

_____

_____

FIVE SOURCES OF EMPLOYEE DEMOTIVATION

- Individual Differences
- Stressful Work
- Organizational Culture
- Conflict Between Co-Workers
- Leadership Style

Chapter 6:

CONFLICT BETWEEN COWORKERS: MY JOB WOULD BE GREAT IF I DIDN'T HAVE TO DEAL WITH CRAZY COWORKERS!

Joanna and Collette were colleagues at a private Christian school. Joanna taught secondary math, and Collette was the assistant administrator. Although they both enjoyed their jobs, Collette and Joanna were polar opposites in the way they interacted with people. Collette was a very cut-and-dried person, whereas Joanna was much more collaborative and approachable. Nearly every time Joanna and Collette interacted, Joanna left feeling disrespected, which poked holes in her motivation basket. Joanna had worked with colleagues who had a very direct communication style in the past, but she felt that Collette frequently crossed the line to the point of being inconsiderate and aggressive. Interestingly, Joanna wasn't the only person in the school who felt that way. Several of Joanna's colleagues avoided Collette and spoke negatively about her communication style. However, because Collette had the longest tenure at the school, no one wanted to broach the topic with her.

One day, Joanna was in Collette's office asking about student grades, which were due in a few days. Joanna knew she needed to approach Collette about a situation with one of her students, but she was afraid of Collette's reaction.

"I have this one student that is going to need some extra time," Joanna said, the butterflies in her stomach going crazy.

"Joanna, it is your responsibility to get those grades in on time," Collette fired back. "If a student is behind and needs more time to finish a certain assignment or test, it's your job to make that up, not mine. Grades are due in two days. All grades. How can your students be held accountable if you're not holding yourself accountable? That's all."

For the first time in all her time dealing with Collette, Joanna couldn't bite her tongue. "Collette, you can't talk to me that way. When you can talk to me as a professional, then we can resume this conversation." With that, Joanna left a stunned Collette sitting in her office sifting through papers.

Back in her classroom, the butterflies continued beating against Joanna's stomach. Fresh out of college, she was a young, eager teacher. What was she thinking confronting an older, more experienced colleague? But as the day wore on, Joanna calmed down. She knew that the time to confront Collette had passed. She also tapped into her higher purpose as a teacher and understood that if she didn't stand up for herself, she wouldn't be able to reach the academic goals that she had set for her students. Later that afternoon, well after the students had been dismissed, Collette walked into Joanna's room and said, "Joanna, let's talk."

The two women sat in Joanna's classroom and talked through each side of the conflict. Joanna explained that she felt like Collette spoke to her as if she were an annoying child. She pointed out specific terminology and instances where Collette's way of communicating made Joanna feel angry, inferior, or picked on. Collette listened first and then asked a few questions so she could really understand where Joanna was coming from. Joanna learned that Collette genuinely had no idea how the way she communicated was bothering Joanna. Based on that conversation, the two women were able to establish boundaries and a sense of mutual respect that allowed them to work together collaboratively from that point forward. They conceded that they viewed appropriate communication differently and agreed to respect the other person's communication style. They also agreed that if they ran into any communication issues or offensive speech going forward, they would handle it immediately instead of waiting for the issue to boil over.

After the conversation, Joanna wondered why she had waited so long to bring the issue before Collette. She wondered why she had waited until she reached a boiling point. Her approach to conflict— that "wait and see if it resolves itself" approach—is common because most people prefer to avoid conflict. In fact, they'll do anything they can to avoid it. Unfortunately, that doesn't work.

TWEET THIS: DON'T BE AFRAID OF CONFLICT AND DON'T IGNORE IT. CONFLICT CAN ACTUALLY WORK.

Now that we've talked about avoiding conflict, let's see how conflict might help.

Tweet this: Don't be afraid of conflict and don't ignore it. Conflict can actually WORK.

When reading this tweet, your initial reaction may be one of skepticism. That doubt is not surprising, given what we may have been taught about conflict, and given our experiences both personal and professional. Conflict, when managed appropriately, can actually be used as a catalyst for change and to improve both individual and organizational performance. In fact, conflict, when managed and leveraged properly, can be functional rather than dysfunctional.

More than one hundred years ago, notable management theorist Mary Parker Follett provided rationale for the benefits of constructive conflict. She asserted that "as conflict—difference—is here in the world, as we cannot avoid it, we should, I think, use it. Instead of condemning it, we should set it to work for us. Why not?" (quoted in Davis 2015).

In a contemporary context, this viewpoint is instructive, because research suggests that employees are reporting increased levels of conflict. In *Managing Workplace Conflict* (2017), the Society for Human Resource Management (SHRM) shares the research of Christine Porath, a noted expert on incivility and associate professor at Georgetown University. In her research, Porath (2016) stated that approximately 25 percent of employees surveyed in 1998 reported they were being treated rudely at work at least once a week. In 2011 that result increased to 55 percent, and by 2016 the figure was 62 percent. Porath asserted that a potential cause for this escalation was a rise in tension related to conflicting political views. In the same publication, SHRM shares a 2015 survey by the Chartered Institute of Personnel and Development, and findings indicated that 40 percent of UK employees reported experiencing some form of interpersonal conflict at work in the past year. Results also indicated that the majority of the conflict was between an employee and his or her line manager. Moreover, the results indicated that employees were more likely to report experiencing conflict with a more senior staff member. Whether it's incivility, bullying, harassment or discrimination, there's a prevalence of conflict in the workplace that organizational leaders must not only understand, but also take concrete steps to effectively resolve.

EMPLOYEES REPORT BEING TREATED RUDELY AT WORK AT LEAST ONCE PER WEEK

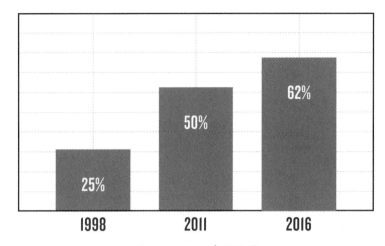

Source: Porath 2016

So, let's define workplace conflict. A contemporary definition is described by Kazimoto (2013), who characterizes workplace conflict as "the presence of discord that occurs when goals, interests or values of different individuals or groups are incompatible and frustrate each other's attempt to achieve objectives in an organization." It's likely that if you've worked in an organization or heard others describe their experiences at work, you've drawn some conclusions about the impact and efficacy of conflict. But it's important to note that conflict can be good and it can be bad. If everyone in a group of people agrees on everything, they may get things done quickly, but without differences, how will innovation come from that group? Innovation, being competitive, thinking outside of the box, and growth all come

> THERE ARE CIRCUMSTANCES IN WHICH CONFLICT CAN BE HEALTHY. IN FACT, SOMETIMES, IT'S GOOD TO "PICK A FIGHT." THE CHALLENGE IS TO KNOW WHICH FIGHTS ARE WORTH FIGHTING.

from conflict. That's the good kind of conflict. Bad conflict occurs when the conflict shuts everybody down from participating. This type of conflict keeps every employee from contributing and is a huge factor in demotivation.

Not all forms of conflict are healthy for the organization, because they sow discord and otherwise create a toxic environment. But there are circumstances in which conflict can be healthy. In fact, sometimes, it's good to "pick a fight." The challenge is to know which fights are worth fighting. Joni and Beyer (2009) assert there are three principles that should inform which fights to pick:

1. **Make it material.** Stakes should be high enough to motivate individuals and should have game-changing potential. This means not fighting over the little things. For example, if Collette had changed the color of the whiteboard markers to a color Joanna didn't like, but the students could see the markers on the board just fine, Collette's decision wouldn't have high enough stakes to initiate a conflict. Joanna was justified in the conflict she did raise with Collette because the result of not having the conflict would negatively impact the long-term outcome of providing an excellent education to her students.

2. **Focus on the future.** Be forward-looking and focus on what's ahead. Future-facing fights shift the focus from what's happened to what could happen. Joanna and Collette both focused on the students and the future when their conflict led to a conversation about boundaries, effective communication styles, and dealing with conflict going forward.

3. **Pursue a noble purpose.** Your fight should be about improving the lives of customers or changing the world for

the better. Focus energies beyond self-interest and on more than money or profits. Joanna approached Collette about her communication style because she knew that her higher purpose, which was to give her kids the best education she could provide, could not be achieved if she did not. If Joanna and Collette weren't colleagues, but were friends instead, and they collided over where to host a birthday party, the conflict might not be addressed because the purpose wouldn't be high enough to force the issue.

In addition to offering a set of guidelines for "what" to fight over, the authors also provide three principles on "how" to fight the right way.

1. **Make it a sport, not a war.** Create rules of the game and then let leaders establish themselves as referees to ensure the rules are followed. A lot of times, people take conflict too far and focus more on winning the war than reaching a middle ground. The conversation becomes more focused on proving Collette is wrong than on reaching an outcome. Sometimes people take this mentality so far that they even get an informal coalition together (think watercooler friends) in order to gang up on the person they don't like. Making conflict a sport is about avoiding a war.

2. **Set up a formal structure, but work informally.** Structure the "fights" in a way that's consistent with formal organizational structures, but also allows employees to leverage personal and professional connections that aren't necessarily reflected in an organizational chart. When Collette and Joanna had their conflict, they agreed on a few things first. They agreed that when they disagree, they will be respectful. They agreed

to always listen to one another and they agreed not to think the worst of each other before, after, or during the conflict. In addition to having a formal structure, we recommend having an informal structure or people who are outside of the department or far from the direct report. These people who aren't necessarily in the hierarchy on the organizational chart can be leveraged as a part of dealing with situations that have come up.

3. **Turn pain into gain.** While we'd like to believe that we can create a "win-win" outcome, the reality is there may be winners and losers. Find a way to turn disappointing news into an opportunity for personal growth and development. Since both Joanna and Collette felt good about the conflict and the outcome, neither had to accept disappointing news. However, conflict often results in negative news for at least one party. Here's an example. Say an employee was going for a vice president position that recently opened and, despite having risen through the ranks, despite having institutional knowledge and having been told they should apply, they don't get it. Although they weren't planning on this news, they know they're going to stay with the company. To turn this conflict into something salvageable, the manager needs to consider how to turn pain into gain. How does the manager support this person? Do they create a new opportunity for the person that supports professional development? Do they help them expand their skill set? Considering these options is what we mean by turning pain into gain. The employee also has a role to play in this situation. They need to look at the disappointing news and figure out how to make it work for them. Do they get more training if they

stay? Is it time for them to make the career change they've been talking about for the last five years?

Because not everything is worth fighting over, establishing a set of guiding principles for "what" and "how" you're going to fight helps to set parameters and expectations for employees. This clarity can be helpful because it provides employees with a framework that informs behavior and creates accountability through the involvement of leadership.

When considering addressing a conflict, it's also useful to know which type of organization you're working within. Just as each of the four organizational cultures we talked about in Chapter 5 handle communication differently, they manage conflict differently. In a hierarchy culture, conflict is often avoided because employees have less decision-making power than within other organizational structures. In a clan culture, because everyone is pretty heavily invested in "the family" feeling, employees might avoid conflict because they don't want anyone in the family to be mad at them. Because a higher value is placed on cohesiveness than innovation and creativity in a clan culture, conflict is often swallowed. Because market cultures are so competitive, conflict is more common. Whenever you have winners and losers and people maneuvering to advance their careers at the expense of others, you'll see more conflict. This could lead to higher turnover. In an adhocracy culture, conflict is desirable, in particular when it serves the goal of innovation, problem-solving, and creativity. People who work in this type of culture likely have habits that invite discord and critical analysis, so conflict is cultivated for its benefits.

It's also worth noting that how an organization approaches conflict is likely influenced by three fundamental attitudes toward conflict reflected in the research of Robbins and Judge (2015). The authors espouse a contemporary view of conflict which asserts three attitudes: traditionalist (believes conflict is inherently negative and should be avoided), human relations (attempts to rationalize the fact that conflict does exist, but doesn't readily embrace it) and interactionist (acknowledges that not all conflict is healthy, but views conflict as essential and therefore encourages opposition and dissenting points of view).

Considering these three attitudes toward conflict, let's see how they work in an organization that's experiencing conflict. A typical decision that can lead to conflict is which person to assign to a high-profile project. Say we have three leaders within one organization sitting around a table trying to decide who to assign. The traditionalist would believe that any conflict brought up in the meeting will be inherently negative and therefore should be avoided. This person may find a formulaic way to figure out who to assign the project to. They may say, "Let's look at each candidate's last performance review," and use an objective process that allows them to avoid having a conversation where people might disagree with each other. The person with the human relations attitude would attempt to rationalize the fact that conflict does in fact exist without readily embracing it. This person might say something like, "Okay, we have to have this conversation, we know it's going to be ugly, I'm not a big fan of it. Let's get it over with and try to minimize the pain." Finally, the interactionist is going to say, "Making decisions like this is one of the reasons that we get paid the big bucks. This is a hard decision and we need to take it seriously. Let's put some ground rules in place and make sure that everybody gets heard." The interactionist might even invite people who are giving off negative body language to speak first about where there's conflict.

It's important to understand the conflicts in your organization as well as your organization's views on conflict because the implications of those viewpoints will affect how employees approach conflict and how they attempt to resolve related issues when they occur. For example, if your organization typically encourages team leaders to have some minimal level of ongoing conflict through debate and critical thinking in order to enhance the efficacy of teams, then the interactionist view is at work.

As you read about conflict between coworkers, it is useful to consider a real situation that you have experienced. Reflect on the last time you personally experienced conflict. What was the nature of the conflict? Think of two other people that you work with who are currently in the middle of a conflict: what's the nature of that particular situation? Is this a recurring type of conflict, or one that you had never faced before? Is this a situation that you anticipated, or did it take you by surprise? Now jot down your thoughts.

Please look at what you wrote. Did you describe conflict related to work assignments, project goals, business decisions about priorities? These can best be described as task conflict. Or did you describe personality clashes, differences in taste, negative emotions or stereotyping? If so, you're referencing relationship conflict.

TASK CONFLICT	RELATIONSHIP CONFLICT
• Differences of opinion about how to do the work • Disagreement about how to allocate resources • Lack of agreement on process, policies, and procedures related to the task • Variability in expectations and goals	• Tension, maybe even animosity, between coworkers • Differences in personality that make it difficult to work together • Incompatibility between colleagues that has a negative effect on interpersonal interactions

Because workplace conflict, whether functional or dysfunctional, is likely to occur, it's important that we understand the negative consequences and their impact. In *Managing Workplace Conflict* (2017), SHRM reports the "negative effects of workplace conflict can include work disruptions, decreased productivity, project failure, absenteeism, turnover, termination and emotional stress." This is why there's a business case to be made for an organization to effectively manage workplace conflict. When these matters are left unresolved, or when they are allowed to escalate, the situation may expose the organization to severe financial consequences because of a tainted reputation, unionization, turnover, absenteeism, and allegations of harassment and discrimination. Given the financial consequences and adverse effect on employees and the organization as a whole, what can companies do to better manage workplace conflict? We have a few ideas of the leadership behaviors that can help with this.

Leadership Actions to Reduce the Demotivating Effect of Workplace Conflict

1. Provide opportunities for employees to learn about their own conflict management styles and work toward developing a wider range of approaches.

2. Assess your own approach to managing conflict, and the impact this has on the employees in your group.

3. Help the team to develop agreements about how to gain value from differences and address the conflict that comes from diverse perspectives.

4. Rather than separating employees who appear to struggle to work together, create more opportunities for collaboration and facilitate agreements to help them recognize the value in working together.

5. Help employees establish norms to keep disagreements focused on the work rather than on emotions and personal differences.

6. Establish an environment of inclusion rather than fostering exclusive relationships within the team.

7. Provide opportunities for the team to build social cohesiveness beyond the work tasks.

8. Establish strong feedback skills so that individuals can effectively communicate concerns with each other directly.

Provide opportunities for employees to learn about their own conflict management styles and work toward developing a wider range of approaches. Self-awareness is a key component of our ability to better manage conflict. So, complete the self-assessment at this link: https://www.usip.org/public-education/students/conflict-styles-assessment. It has thirty questions and takes about ten to fifteen minutes to complete. The assessment was developed by the United States Institute of Peace and is based upon the Thomas Kilmann instrument, which is used by HR professionals around the world. The assessment includes five conflict management styles and will help employees to develop an understanding of their natural tendencies when responding to conflict. This awareness will also help them to better understand the styles of others, so they are more adept in resolving conflicts.

Assess your own approach to managing conflict, and the impact this has on the employees in your group. It's important that employees understand the important role that they play in managing workplace conflict. Managers can assist in this process by coaching employees on how to talk to their peers directly when a conflict surfaces. There are plenty of resources available to help a manager develop these skills in their employees, but the informal coaching relationship between a leader and their employees is a very important part of the process. Here's a follow-up exercise for self-assessment that can be completed individually or with employees. Return to the situation between Joanna and Colette at the beginning of this chapter, and put yourself in Joanna's shoes. Based on what you just assessed in the online tool, if you were Joanna, how would you approach it? What does this teach you about the different choices you have in conflict styles? Pick a style other than your own. How would you approach it? Conflict management isn't a one-size-fits-all proposition. So, the exercise is intended to be illustrative and to help you not only think through your style preference, but better understand its strengths and weaknesses and how it affects others. In doing so, it's our hope that you will be able to better respond to conflict when it invariably presents itself.

Help the team to develop agreements about how to gain value from differences and address the conflict that comes from diverse perspectives. Because conflict is inevitable in teamwork, it is useful to begin discussing the value of differences and the approach to managing conflict before the conflict even arises. As a leader, you can facilitate a discussion that leads to agreements about how conflict will be handled, which will come in handy as a tool to refer to when actual conflicts arise. As noted with Collette and Joanna, establishing boundaries and expectations for how to address conflict can be a useful tool for handling it.

Rather than separating employees who appear to struggle to work together, create more opportunities for collaboration and facilitate agreements to help them recognize the value in working together. In our experiences, we have found many people default to the model of separating people who seem to struggle to work together. The problem with that approach is that everyone on the team has to dance around the fact that the conflict exists, and this dance takes a lot of energy away from the actual work. Avoiding the conflict by separating people has the effect of demotivating the entire team, so it is far better to create circumstances that cause the conflicting employees to work out their differences. Managers can assist in this process by coaching employees on talking to their peers directly when a conflict surfaces.

Help employees establish norms to keep disagreements focused on the work rather than on emotions and personal differences. Oftentimes when two people are experiencing conflict, other people see it, but the people involved don't. Leaders and managers can see that others are having conflict and use that as a coaching opportunity then and there. They might say something like, "Hey, Bob, it looks like you and Sam are really having a hard time hearing each other on this taskforce. Are you noticing that? What could you differently, Bob? How can I help you think about different approaches you might take so Sam hears you and you're listening to him more?" You might consider having your team complete the self-assessment on conflict management styles and then have the group discuss their results. This could be followed by a role-playing exercise where each team member picks a style different from their own in responding to the conflict. Then debrief.

Establish an environment of inclusion rather than fostering exclusive relationships within the team. Just as it is common to find people who clash when working together, it is also common to find people who have great chemistry as coworkers. The problem within a team is that the closeness of a small "in-group," while very motivating to those in it, can have a very demotivating impact on those who are left in the "out-group." It is important as a leader to create opportunities for all of the members of the team to build cohesive working relationships, which requires careful nurturing that goes beyond the immediate friendships that some coworkers build to the exclusion of others.

Provide opportunities for the team to build social cohesiveness beyond the work tasks. People who like working together are far more effective in completing the goals of the team than people who don't like each other. This cohesiveness can come from the great communication and respect that arises from working well on tasks together, or it can come from building social bonds that go beyond the job. As a leader, it is important to help your team find opportunities to build social cohesiveness, which can include small activities such as celebrating work anniversaries or other events during work hours, or bigger activities that involve getting out of the office for a little team-building fun. When people are more cohesive, they handle conflict more effectively, so it is a worthwhile investment for maintaining the motivation of all of the team.

Establish strong feedback skills so that individuals can effectively communicate concerns with each other directly. Helping employees learn to manage conflict not only empowers the employee, but also frees the manager from the added responsibility of refereeing every employee conflict that may surface. This doesn't mean the manager isn't an arbiter when circumstances warrant. But this does provide an outlet for employees to resolve their own conflicts without management intervention where possible.

Now that you have a better understanding of ideas that leaders can use to help employees manage conflict, let's take a look at two examples of leaders who have tried different approaches, and the impact that these approaches had on motivation and demotivation for their teams.

One of the coolest learning experiences that we have encountered is something we do with our MBA students at Northwood University every summer in the form of management leadership simulations. We put people in leadership roles on simulated teams and they spend a week running these mock organizations. It's a very high-intensity environment for them interpersonally as well as internally because they're practicing the actual skills it takes to be successful in making decisions that need to be made in order to run a company. These students come from various campuses, so they also don't know each other. They represent diversity in age, race, and professional backgrounds, so there's plenty of opportunity for conflict among them. To start the simulated experience, we assign them each to various roles, including leadership roles, and they have to work together for a week competing with other teams.

Each simulation team is running a company that competes in a fictitious computer industry. The groups are responsible for manufacturing and selling personal computers. As part of the process of designing a computer, they also have to answer questions such as: How much inventory should their organization keep? Will they manufacture a high-end product or a low-end product? How will they decide the price of that product? Will they advertise or not? How many salespeople do they need?

During one of these simulations, Kendall, who was the president of Team A, ran into conflict right away. In the very first group decisions, there were people who wanted to assert their authority and power. They were vocal about their own need for control but not interested in hearing anybody else's point of view. Kendall didn't quite know how to handle it. As you can imagine, many students who participate in these simulations have Type A personalities. They are used to getting their way, they're not afraid to speak up, and they like having control. Well, when a few of these students started disagreeing about the overall strategy for this company's growth, Kendall got run over. He found himself sitting there listening to three other people lead the team. The other people in the room who were less vocal began to show that they were frustrated and checked out. Before long, the conversation started going around in circles with no leadership from Kendall.

The simulation had divided the team into three departments: finance, marketing, and operations. After the meeting, everyone returned to their own department. The people in the marketing department continued the strategy conversation among themselves. As they had these discussions, they tore down people who were not in the room and completely undermined any direction Kendall had presented during the company-wide meeting. As the days wore on, the marketing department continued on its own path. Not only were they negative in every communication with any other department, but they were disrespectful of Kendall. In the few company meetings that took place following marketing's spinoff, no one said much. Most of Kendall's employees felt that they didn't have direction, that nothing they said mattered, and that if they brought up any issues, Kendall wouldn't have the power to do anything about it. Therefore, they would look at their laptops or scroll through their phones, both clear physical displays of demotivation.

As you can imagine, Team A's results weren't great. In fact, their results were average at best. The company was barely profitable, its market share was low, and the overall company ranking was in the bottom 25 percent. When asked to review their experience at the end of the week, everyone on Team A said that they had "survived" the experience. Many of them had learned a lot about their own tasks. Many of them liked the people in their department, but they otherwise described the entire week as frustrating and stressful. Kendall had never handled any decisions, leading to ambiguity, and the ambiguity caused them to make bad business decisions.

While Kendall's results were not good, his colleague, Kevin, had great results. Going into the simulation as a team president, Kevin had similar challenges. He was working with high-performing MBA students who had different experiences. They were used to being in control and had Type A personalities. Like with Kendall's team, Kevin's team (Team B) entered the project with full motivation baskets. However, Kevin didn't blast holes in their motivation baskets because, unlike Kendall, he dealt with the conflicts that arose immediately.

When Team B members started voicing their concerns about Kevin's strategy, Kevin created space and time for them to raise their issues. As soon as his team started expressing conflicting ideas, Kevin said, "It's great that we have so much energy! Of course, because we're twelve different people, we're going to have different points of view, so let's make some deals about how to handle them."

Then Kevin had the team establish some ground rules around how they would interact. Those rules stipulated that whenever someone didn't like something or didn't agree with someone else, they wouldn't talk behind other team members' backs. Instead, they would bring the issue up and address it head-on. This created boundaries around how the team would talk to each other and resolve issues. Whenever conflict or debate arose, everyone had a chance to be heard, a communication style was adhered to, and they were given a timeline for voicing their concerns so that when the debate was over, it was over and a decision was immediately made. As a result, whenever there was conflict within the departments about Team B's general direction, other team members would say, "No, we're not going down that path. We said this would work, so that's what we're going to do." Because Kevin was willing to work with conflict from the get-go, the smaller teams within his organization ended up with peer accountability, which had never developed in Kendall's group.

Another thing that Kevin did well was check in with his team. Throughout the week, he gauged the mood of his team by watching their body posture and listening to the words and tones they used in conversation. This way, he was able to address conflict and demotivation immediately.

Even though both Kevin's and Kendall's teams had plenty of conflict, Kevin's team had better outcomes because processes were put in place from the start of the simulation to ensure that conflict would be dealt with appropriately. Kevin's team could own the tweet "Don't be afraid of conflict and don't ignore it. Conflict can actually work, you just need to know how to address it."

Whether you're Kendall or Kevin, each of us has the opportunity to grow and develop. So take a look at the leadership behaviors we've previously recommended in this chapter. Then pick a couple that you have some energy for and would like to work on, so that you can make the most of conflict between the various people who work together in your organization.

REFLECTION:

Consider how you address conflict in your organization. Then take a look at the eight leadership action items on page 109 that can help keep you from further demotivating employees. Write down two that you would like to start doing.

_____

_____

_____

_____

_____

_____

FIVE SOURCES OF
EMPLOYEE
DEMOTIVATION

- Individual Differences

- Stressful Work

- Organizational Culture

- Conflict Between Co-Workers

- Leadership Style

Chapter 7:

LEADERSHIP STYLE: ARE PEOPLE LEAVING YOU OR THE COMPANY?

Mike held the position of vice president of operations for the Nashville division of Sam's Sporting Goods stores, which included six retail stores spread out across the metropolitan neighborhoods surrounding Nashville. Each of the retail stores had a store manager who reported to Mike, and the group met regularly to coordinate policies and procedures, share resources, and sort through problems together. Mike traveled to each of the six stores on a regular basis, and he had phone calls with each store manager at least once a day. The store managers were required to run all major decisions by Mike, and he would get upset if he learned that something had happened that he did not know about in advance. When Mike had all six store managers in meetings together, he did most of the talking, although he often referred to "we" to give the appearance that the rest of the managers had something to offer to the group decisions. When Mike asked for input during these meetings, he was quick to shut down the ideas provided, so the managers learned not to speak up unless they were agreeing with him, which made the meetings go by more quickly. For the most part, the managers believed these meetings were a waste of time, and they came to understand that nobody really respected Mike. The only good thing that came of these group meetings is that the six store managers would head out for a beer after the meetings were over, and they became pretty good friends.

The six store managers had regular interaction (mostly by phone) during the work week, although they did not share that with Mike, because he believed that he should be involved in all communications. Mike did not seem to trust anyone, and he was very quick to talk about other store managers when having one-on-one conversations. He mostly pointed out their flaws, so it left each store manager wondering what was being said behind their backs.

Not surprisingly, there was a lot of turnover among the store managers, and they all helped each other out in searching for and moving to new retail store management opportunities in the area. Mike explained this away as a compensation decision, but the store managers all knew that they just hated working for Mike.

> IT IS IN EVERYONE'S BEST INTEREST FOR WORKERS TO BE HIGHLY MOTIVATED AND PRODUCTIVE, AND MOST BOSSES RECOGNIZE THAT; THEY JUST DON'T SEE THE WAY IN WHICH THEIR BEHAVIOR IS IMPACTING THEIR EMPLOYEES.

If you have ever worked for a person like Mike, you know how demotivating it is to interact with someone who does not trust you, talks about you behind your back, and seems not to be interested in anyone's ideas but his own.

It may surprise you to learn that we don't really blame the Mikes out there for messing up your work life. We recognize that these bosses play a significant role in your motivational journey, but we don't presume that it is their goal to have a negative impact on their workers. It is in everyone's best interest for workers to be highly motivated and productive, and most bosses recognize that; they just don't see the way in which their behavior is impacting their employees. Some managers don't know which behaviors they should be looking for. They don't know to look for personal factors, conditions of stress, how people are getting along with each other, and the organizational culture, and how conflict is managed within that culture. Other managers look in the wrong place to determine which types of behaviors they should be using in order to achieve maximum productivity from their workers. In other words, they look at what everyone else is doing wrong instead of what they're doing to affect the situation. There are dozens of reasons this is the case, and a number of ways that the behavior of the boss can be modified, which will be the focus of this chapter.

There are a few versions of this well-known saying, and we choose to quote Marcus Buckingham and Curt Coffman in reinforcing the fact that "people leave managers, not companies" (1999). Sure, there are aspects of a company that attract a person, and there are industries and organizational cultures that have an impact on the decision to join a company, to stick around for a while, and to thrive in that organization. But nothing impacts an employee's motivation more than the behavior of their bosses.

Managers and leaders play a really important role in the life of a worker. Among many other things, it is the boss who is responsible for providing clear direction on what the worker must deliver, and oftentimes they need to provide parameters that direct how the work is done as well as what the final product looks like. They need to help us understand why the work matters and what the big picture goals are. They need to communicate a wide range of things that we need to know in order to do our jobs, and frequently we need bosses to help us remove obstacles that are in the way of completing our tasks. They give us valuable information about how we are doing and push us to expand our skills and develop into other roles at work.

They advocate on our behalf with other folks in the organization in order to make sure that we have adequate resources to complete our work and that we have influence within the organization. When all of these things are done well, the result is a trusting and productive relationship. When some or all of these things are broken, it plays a significant role in demotivating employees.

Many scholars have examined the behaviors of leadership, and there is no shortage of models and theories that you could explore in order to determine the best approach to leading others; we will be introducing you to some of those ideas within this chapter as we examine very specific behaviors that workers need from their leaders. All of these behaviors exist inside models and theories that have been well developed, and we chose these specifically based on our experiences and understanding of their impact on motivation. We have framed these behaviors as failures because, when leaders overlook these specific employee needs, the impact on employee demotivation is significant. These important behaviors are as follows.

Failures of Leadership

1. Failure to Explain the Why
2. Failure to Communicate Frequently and Clearly
3. Failure to Invite Input and Opinions
4. Failure to Provide Effective Feedback and Coaching
5. Failure to Remove Obstacles
6. Failure to Adjust Leadership Styles

While the previous chapters have discussed how leaders can contribute to other sources of demotivation, such as organizational structure and workplace stress, the leader him- or herself can be a demotivating factor entirely on their own. This is why we have chosen to closely examine each of the next six actions as failures to provide leadership behaviors that employees need. To illustrate each of the six failures, we will be sharing the story of Ian's leadership journey, which will primarily show a lot of good choices that Ian makes as a leader. The examples of how Ian understands and addresses the various needs of employees are contrasted with an explanation of what happens when a leader fails in each of these six categories.

FAILURE TO EXPLAIN THE WHY

One of the first things Ian did when he took over as CEO of a commercial real estate company that owned several hotels in the southwest was travel to each of the company's five headquarters and each of its hotels so that he could share his vision of where he wanted the company to go with everyone in the organization. During those open meetings, Ian talked about the new markets that he wanted to pursue, the new approach to customer service he wanted to take, and what he expected in terms of corporate-wide outcomes. He also told everyone within the company that he would fight for the things they needed to get their jobs done. When Ian made that promise, when he said he would do his best to get the obstacles removed that were preventing his employees from doing their jobs, everyone thought, "Okay, I can support this."

Ian's commitment to sharing his vision with his new employees on his first day on the job energized everyone in the organization. It gave them each a sense of where they were going. It gave them a road map so they knew what was expected of them. His passion for his vision reinforced their own commitment to the company.

Now, as you may have experienced, not all managers approach their first few weeks on the job the way Ian did. Some leaders only have meetings with high level executives and board members. They start their time with the organization without ever really interacting with anyone else or gathering any ideas from others. Maybe they don't want to rock the boat. Maybe they're used to only working with higher level employees. Or maybe they don't want to meet a lot of people until they know more about the organization, because they don't want everyone to see that they don't have it all figured out right away. Whatever the case, it's much better for a leader to communicate a vision than it is to leave the direction of an organization ambiguous and vague.

In some cases, a leader might share his or her vision and then not put the resources behind the activities that need to be done to achieve that vision. Ian assures his employees that he won't do that when he promises to give them resources to do their jobs and then does just that.

Quite a lot has been written about the importance of helping people know the why behind the goals and activities of their jobs.

Simon Sinek makes a compelling case in his book "Start with Why," where he explains that the job of leaders is to inspire people to act. He goes on to say that inspiring people gives them a "sense of purpose that has little to do with external incentives" to do the work that they were hired to do (Sinek 2009). This sense of purpose has a very powerful impact on motivation. We can rise to a challenge in the service of a purpose, which allows us to focus, fight our way through obstacles, and feel a sense of pride that is not readily available when we do things that we regard as purposeless. In their theory and research on Transformational Leadership, Bernard Bass and Bruce Aviolo have identified a component of their model as "Inspirational Motivation," to refer to the impact of a leader expressing a vision that is appealing to followers (Bass 1990). A robust body of supporting research demonstrates the highest levels of employee satisfaction and other positive workplace outcomes that are associated with working for a boss who uses the inspirational motivation behaviors.

Daniel Goleman also studied the impact of different leadership behaviors on outcomes for their followers and found that the set of behaviors that he

> WE CAN RISE TO A CHALLENGE IN THE SERVICE OF A PURPOSE, WHICH ALLOWS US TO FOCUS, FIGHT OUR WAY THROUGH OBSTACLES, AND FEEL A SENSE OF PRIDE THAT IS NOT READILY AVAILABLE WHEN WE DO THINGS THAT WE REGARD AS PURPOSELESS.

referred to as "Visionary" (originally labeled as "Authoritative" in his model) had a positive impact on the climate of the organization, which indicates that people who are clearly focused on the purpose of the work have the best outcomes (Goleman 2000). The expression of vision is especially important when people are experiencing change in their environment. This is reinforced by the work of John Kotter (1996), who included establishing a vision as well as creating a sense of urgency (the why) as two of the eight important behaviors for leaders to use for successful change management.

What happens to workers with a boss who does not express a vision or purpose the way Ian did? They are likely to be able to perform the jobs that they were hired to do and form meaningful relationships with coworkers and others, and may be perfectly happy for as long as things stay in the predictable space of the status quo. Others will be overwhelmed by the effort it takes to sort through all of the assumptions that people make about why something matters, and they may find it frustrating to adjust their goals and activities based on this ambiguity. They may adopt a neutral attitude about their company, with a level of commitment that resembles a sense of obligation or even a feeling that they are trapped in the job. As we discussed in Chapter 3, these types of commitments are referred to as normative commitment (sense of obligation) and continuance commitment (feeling trapped), and tend to starve a person of the type of motivation that comes with affective commitment, which essentially refers to the love one has for the work that one does and the organization that one works for (Mowday et al. 1982).

Many organizational leaders participate in strategic planning meetings in which a vision, mission, values, or other types of organizational directives are designed. These are great, provided that they are communicated to the employees, and as long as the vision and mission speak to meaningful things that the employee believes he contributes to and the leaders "walk the talk." We have experienced too many situations in which a motivated employee loses faith in their leader when they see that the leader says one thing while doing another. For example, we once consulted with the leader of a healthcare organization that put a lot of energy into strategic planning. Much time and resources were invested in coming up with a set of vision, mission, and strategic goals for the organization. The CEO and upper-level management created a list of the behaviors that they, as leaders, wanted everyone to focus on as a part of their strategic goals. One of those things on the list was accountability, but the CEO constantly dodged accountability and placed blame on other people for not achieving company-wide goals. In addition to this, the CEO constantly talked about teamwork, sharing resources, and collaborating, yet he notoriously made it difficult for his employees to share resources and he also pitted them against each other. This caused enormous chaos within the organization and poked holes in the employees' motivation baskets.

FAILURE TO COMMUNICATE FREQUENTLY AND CLEARLY

The second behavior of leadership refers to the frequency and clarity of communication. When Ian started his job, he made communication a priority beyond the initial meeting he had with everyone to explain his vision. Twice a month, Ian visited each of the eleven hotel properties that the company owned in the southwest. When he was there, he didn't just have meetings with the executives and the managers. He also wandered around to check the pulse of his organization. He chatted with the housekeeping staff and got to know what was important to them. He hung out near the kitchen so he could talk to the waitstaff and spent time in reception talking to the front desk staff. Ian established a policy of informal communication that went outside of a formal chain of command. This made his employees more willing to share their thoughts, ideas, and concerns with him. These conversations also made Ian's employees feel good because when he walked through the hotels, he often openly praised them in front of their peers.

Leaders tend to be very busy people, and they sometimes miss the opportunity to provide information that is useful to the employees in making decisions and completing their tasks. When people don't get the information they need, they tend to make stuff up, which has a very destructive impact on the norms and the culture in the organization. If Ian had approached communication the way Mike did in Chapter 5, his employees would have heard very little about the organization. Rumor mills fill the gaps in information with guesses that tend to be inaccurate and almost always paint a negative picture.

The frequency of communication a leader has with staff correlates strongly with workplace satisfaction among employees for many pragmatic reasons, but mostly because it causes employees to feel valued and engaged. Taking the time to share information and news (in person, when possible, or in other forms) is a small act that has a great impact on employee motivation.

Among the many theories of leadership that have been presented over the years, one behavior finds its way into nearly every model (with a range of labels), which is that leaders need to clearly communicate their expectations. People who have to worry about whether they are doing the right work, or doing the work incorrectly, or what is coming next and how will it be measured, become paralyzed with fear. They spend too much time talking to others to get the clarity that they need to do their jobs, and they approach with caution, trying to be sure that they don't mess up. Fear is a great demotivator, and is something that can be avoided by simply taking the time to clearly communicate your expectations. When communication is a two-way street, then employees get to demonstrate their commitment and expertise and engagement, all of which feed their motivation. If a boss shows an interest in what the employee is doing, thinking, or worrying about, then employees feel the sense of value that enables them to continue to be motivated to contribute more and perform at the highest level. This leads us to the third leadership behavior on the list.

FEAR IS A GREAT DEMOTIVATOR, AND IS SOMETHING THAT CAN BE AVOIDED BY SIMPLY TAKING THE TIME TO CLEARLY COMMUNICATE YOUR EXPECTATIONS. WHEN COMMUNICATION IS A TWO-WAY STREET, THEN EMPLOYEES GET TO DEMONSTRATE THEIR COMMITMENT AND EXPERTISE AND ENGAGEMENT, ALL OF WHICH FEED THEIR MOTIVATION.

FAILURE TO INVITE INPUT AND OPINIONS

Not long after Ian started his job as CEO, his company started designing another hotel. Instead of only asking for input from his leadership team, Ian asked everyone in the organization to provide feedback on the design. He asked the housekeeping staff what the executive team could do better in terms of designing the room layout and found out that putting nightstands too close to the beds made it extremely difficult to make the beds. He asked the kitchen staff to help design the new kitchen from scratch. From them, he learned that the flow of cabinetry and tools in the existing kitchens could have been designed in a better way. By asking for his employees' opinions, not only was Ian able to create a better outcome, but he also got buy-in from his employees. It's really easy to complain about decisions that didn't involve your input and much harder to complain when your input was asked for. It should be noted here that if a suggestion is asked for and then not followed through on, the leader should explain why the decision was made the way it was. This is called closing the feedback loop. This is where you go back to people and you let them know what happened. You say, "Guys, this is a great idea, but here's why we couldn't do it." When the feedback loop is closed, people are generally grateful that they mattered enough to be consulted on the decision and less concerned about whether their idea was used.

The findings of Gallup's survey of employee engagement reinforce the importance of this leadership behavior. The survey has twelve elements of engagement that are presented as questions. The seventh question is "At work, my opinions seem to count." This engagement element is consequential because it measures the employees' sense of inclusion and value. When employees are listened to and given a voice to provide suggestions and input, they feel a sense of appreciation and buy-in for decisions that are made. As a result, when leaders are contemplating or implementing change in the organization, "employees want to know that their input is being considered and encouraged and that they can voice their opinion without fear of retaliation" (Gallup 2017c).

Data from the Gallup 2017 State of the American Workplace Report found that 30 percent of employees in the United States "strongly agree" with the seventh engagement element (Gallup 2017a). So, why should leaders be concerned with improving this metric? Well, there's a financial benefit for the organization. By doubling the ratio from 30 percent to 60 percent, Gallup's research has found that a firm may be able to increase productivity by 12 percent and reduce employee turnover by 27 percent (ibid.). Productivity and turnover are excellent measures of increases in employee motivation, as well as a reversal of employee demotivation as fewer people get fed up and quit the company.

Given the financial ramifications and the need to recruit and retain highly talented employees, what are the best leaders doing?

- Promoting open, creative dialogue
- Encouraging new ideas that can positively influence business results
- Providing open and honest feedback on opinions and ideas, advocating for good ones and addressing unfeasible ones
- Creating feedback loops so employees feel involved in decision-making processes
- Proactively ensuring employees understand how a situation resolves after they offer an opinion or suggestion, as well as why a recommendation may not be possible to implement.

As you look through the above list, are there any aspects of communicating with employees that you need to work on? Can you identify which play to your strengths and which play to your weaknesses?

Of the four cultures we discussed in Chapter 5, inviting input and opinions works in every culture except for the hierarchy culture, where decisions are made at the top and then carried out throughout the rest of the organization. In this type of organization, employees can still feel like they have a voice if the leader says something like, "There will be a hierarchy decision, but we'd still like to hear your input." Sometimes just being upfront helps employees understand and appreciate what's happening within the organization.

FAILURE TO PROVIDE EFFECTIVE FEEDBACK AND COACHING

When Ian started his job, one of the hotels wasn't doing very well. Ian knew he'd have to speak with Taylor, the general manager of that hotel, about the issue in order to determine what was happening and what needed to be done to improve performance. Before talking with Taylor, Ian made a point to observe a little bit more about the property.

For several days, Ian stayed at the struggling hotel. He worked side by side with Taylor and observed some specific behaviors. Taylor didn't get out and talk to her employees very much, she was annoyed when people came to her with problems, and there seemed to be some morale issues in the hotel. Ian also noticed that once word was out that he was at the hotel, numerous employees wanted to talk to him about Taylor and the way she managed. Instead of encouraging this chatter, Ian decided to talk to Taylor himself.

When Ian sat down with Taylor, he learned that she knew everyone was intimidated by her, but that she was following the lead of her last boss, who had led by fear, and doing what she thought was expected of a general manager. Ian then talked to Taylor about her leadership style and made suggestions as to how she might improve her communication with employees. He told Taylor how her interactions made him feel. He didn't attack her or tell her that she had an aggressive management style. He simply stated his experience with her. Ian's approach gave Taylor information about how her communication affected others and what she could do about it. It also gave her an opportunity to hear where he was coming from and then explore his way of doing things. In addition to talking to her, he agreed to meet with her every other week so he could check in and see how things were going.

Ian handled this situation better than some CEOs. Other leaders might have spent their time talking to the employees about Taylor, or they might have fired her on the spot based on one bad meeting and the observations made about the hotel's performance. Neither of these approaches would have allowed Taylor to grow as a leader.

Feedback is a very specific form of communication that is important for leaders. It's also the first stage of coaching an employee for improved performance. When a leader provides effective feedback, they are making an investment in the employee. Unless it is delivered poorly (more on that later), effective feedback can significantly impact the trust and commitment of workers, even when the feedback is about something that the employee did incorrectly. It is easy for all of us to talk about people, but it takes a specific level of skill and concern to talk to people directly about their performance. Because we all know that feedback conversations are difficult, we appreciate when someone goes to the effort of helping us out by providing their feedback to us. When we recognize the gift of feedback that we are receiving from our leader, it inspires us to make the effort to make changes and improve.

For most of us, giving corrective feedback is the most challenging, but it is also likely that we walk past the opportunity to give positive feedback, because we feel uncomfortable, or because we assume that our employees already know how great they are. People need both types of feedback and are more likely to trust your message and your intent if they get useful feedback about both positive and negative behaviors, delivered in a timely manner, so that they have a legitimate chance of making improvements. In addition to timeliness, the tone and goal of feedback must clearly display the leader's intention to provide help, rather than an evaluation or judgment of the worker. The goal in delivering feedback is to reduce any awkwardness and defensiveness on the part of the employee receiving it. If done effectively, it can build trust and open dialogue between the employee and the leader.

Because delivering feedback creates an uncomfortable interpersonal dynamic, with the risk of straining the relationship by offending someone or being misunderstood, many leaders avoid giving performance feedback other than through the formal performance review process. When we don't give feedback to people on a regular basis, they can become complacent or may feel uncertainty about where they stand in the leader's eyes. These worries and frustrations are draining on the motivation that employees might otherwise be applying to their work, so it is important for the leader to step up and communicate. When feedback happens with frequency, it takes out the sting and the awkwardness that might otherwise be present in the discussion. The employee gets useful information on a regular basis, and this builds a trusting relationship between employee and manager.

The process of giving feedback naturally leads to coaching opportunities, which have the purpose of helping the employee to build more confidence and/or competence with new or challenging tasks. Some leaders have an interest in coaching their employees but cannot make the investment of time that it takes, so this is often a missed opportunity. Unfortunately, this leaves the employee with confidence and/or competence deficiencies, and that vulnerability is another thing that eats away at their motivation.

FAILURE TO REMOVE OBSTACLES

During the construction of the hotel that Ian had helped design, he had to figure out how to meet the really aggressive completion deadlines set by the former CEO. In addition to that obstacle, Ian also had to figure out ways staff could meet those deadlines while also working on the projects they were already managing. To do this, Ian worked with a supplier so one aspect of the project could move along more quickly. He also shifted workloads and projects so those who needed to focus on building the new hotel could do just that.

A manager who doesn't step in to remove obstacles that prevent employees from succeeding, but still holds their employees accountable for meeting deadlines and producing good results, will shoot many holes in their employees' motivation baskets.

Another result of the frequent communication, feedback, and coaching interactions between employees and their bosses is the opportunity to help the employee solve problems and overcome obstacles. Sometimes these obstacles are outside of the employee's control. They may not know how to manage their time well or have to take on projects that are over their head because they haven't developed the skills needed to tackle them yet, or they may have too much on their plate. This is an area in which employees need the support of their leaders to help navigate the politics and address obstacles that are out of their reach. If a leader leaves the employees to fend for themselves, their motivation is likely to waver as they experience greater difficulty and frustration associated with navigating these murky waters.

Of course, sometimes our obstacles are self-imposed, based on various personal factors that we discussed in Chapter 3. For example, a person who is not open to experience is likely going to resist everything naturally, which is an obstacle. A negative disposition could also be an obstacle within the employee's control.

Some leaders fail to take action to remove obstacles, either because they lack organizational power or take a conservative risk posture, which may lead to missed opportunities for the department or organization as a whole. This is very frustrating for employees, who may not have the access or position power that they need to fight for resources or to make sure that the goals of the department receive the proper attention. In the transformation leadership theory, this specific style is referred to as "Laissez-Faire" leadership, which essentially is a hands-off approach to leadership (Bass 1990). Many people like the idea that their boss is not interfering with the day-to-day activities of their job, but a boss who is not involved at all is even more demotivating, because important things do not get addressed.

FAILURE TO ADJUST LEADERSHIP STYLES

When Ian was providing feedback and coaching to help Taylor improve her own leadership approaches, he was recognizing her challenges and adjusting his behavior to help her. He was spending some extra energy and time with Taylor, observing and then engaging her in discussion to help her learn, then listening as she sorted through her struggles and providing helpful feedback. This is referred to as a coaching style by several leadership style theorists, including Daniel Goleman (2000) and Ken Blanchard (Blanchard et al. 2013). There are a lot of other leadership behaviors that Ian could have chosen to use with Taylor, and there was a time that Ian would likely have flexed his power and used a coercive or directing style to tell her to "shape up or ship out" in the role that she had been messing up. But Ian understood that he needed to make sure he approached his employees with different leadership styles that best fit the variety of situations that they faced in completing their jobs.

With his model of Situational Leadership, Ken Blanchard is among the leading advocates for the idea that leaders need to diagnose the varied needs of employees, which requires understanding employees' competence and commitment (motivation) for their tasks (ibid.). The model offers the leader a range of styles that should be used to match their diagnosis, including directing, coaching, supporting and delegating styles. Daniel Goleman (2000) extended his research on the construct of emotional intelligence to consider the impact of six different leadership styles on employees, which included the following:

- Coercive or Commanding (telling employees what to do)
- Authoritative or Visioning (inspiring employees toward a vision or goal)
- Affiliative (interacting with employees and demonstrating

genuine interest in them)

- Democratic (engaging all employees and soliciting input in decision-making)
- Pacesetter (contributing high levels of expertise and effort in completing tasks)
- Coaching (investing in the development of employee skills)

In working with thousands of leaders on their own development, we have been surprised at the number of leaders who resist the idea of flexing their leadership behaviors to meet the needs of their employees. The general sentiment is "I am who I am," as if to say that people must adjust to them, rather than the leader adjusting to the people. These leaders struggle to let go of the behaviors that they believe earned them their leadership role, and they see it as a sign of weakness to try new behaviors that may not be as natural as the behaviors that they have been fine-tuning for many years. They may have developed leadership behaviors by modeling the behaviors of their role models, or they may have strongly-held beliefs about leading others based on wisdom that has been passed down from respected others. All of these compete with the idea that they need to read the needs of employees and adjust their own leadership approach to meet those needs.

The research conducted by Goleman provides very specific insight into the impact of these leadership behaviors on employees, which may provide useful information to those who are considering whether or not to make the effort to develop additional approaches to leadership. While the research suggests that all of the leadership styles in Goleman's model are appropriate for certain situations, overuse of any of these styles may have demotivating effects on employees. Imagine if you worked for a leader who only used a commanding leadership style, which is likely great when there is a crisis or major safety concerns in an emergency situation, but could quickly burn out the employees who feel demotivated by the fact that they simply take orders and do not participate in any problem-solving or decision-making for their jobs. Similarly, we may find that a

---

EMPLOYEE COMMITMENT IS MOST STRONGLY CORRELATED WITH THE LEADERSHIP STYLES OF VISIONARY (AUTHORITATIVE) AND AFFILIATIVE LEADERS, AND THE COACHING AND DEMOCRATIC STYLES ALSO SHOW A STRONG CORRELATION. IT IS LIKELY THAT EMPLOYEES REGARD THESE LEADERSHIP BEHAVIORS AS SHOWING AN INTEREST IN THEM AND THEIR SUCCESS...

---

pacesetter style of leadership is very impressive, because the leader is rolling up their sleeves and bringing their expertise to the work, and it is likely that the application of the leader's expertise leads to very good outcomes. However, if you hang out with a pacesetter leader, you will likely become demotivated rather quickly, because you do not have their level of expertise or contribution, which impacts your own sense of accomplishment.

Employee commitment is most strongly correlated with the leadership styles of visionary (authoritative) and affiliative leaders, and the coaching and democratic styles also show a strong correlation. It is likely that employees regard these leadership behaviors as showing an interest in them and their success, providing inspiration, engaging them, and supporting their development. The best outcomes for employee motivation come from the flexible use of various leadership styles, and it is important to recognize what employees need from you if you are going to be successful at helping them to repair the holes in their baskets of motivation.

During this chapter, we introduced six failures in leadership behaviors that affect employee demotivation. Based upon our professional experiences and the research, these failures are consequential because of their impact on employees and organizational performance. Therefore, it's important that leaders figure out how to close the gap. Since these leadership behaviors are all examined as *failures* to behave, the implication is that leaders need to recognize and implement all six of these important actions in order to avoid demotivating their employees. For the sake of consistency, and also to end on a positive note, we have reworded all of these leadership failures to indicate the appropriate leadership actions that impact employee demotivation in the chart below.

Leadership Actions That Impact Demotivation of Employees Overall

1. Explain the Why
2. Communicate Frequently and Clearly
3. Invite Input and Opinions
4. Provide Effective Feedback and Coaching
5. Remove Obstacles
6. Use a Range of Leadership Styles

REFLECTION:

As you think about your own approaches and challenges, which of these behaviors represent opportunities for you to improve? Based upon ideas presented in the chapter, what action steps are you planning to pursue and when? Take a few minutes to write down your responses to these questions in the reflection box provided below.

_____

_____

_____

_____

_____

_____

Chapter 8:

WHAT CAN A LEADER DO TO PREVENT OR REPAIR DEMOTIVATION?

Do you remember the outstanding young leader Amanda who was a bright star at the car dealership she worked for until her manager and a change in company culture started blasting holes in her motivation basket? We introduced you to Amanda during the introduction to *The Demotivated Employee*. As a recap, Amanda moved into a leadership role at her car dealership after completing a leadership development training program. She knew a lot about cars and was exceptionally skilled at providing outstanding customer service. Every day Amanda greeted her job early with a big smile and lots of ideas. Not long after Amanda took on the role of used car sales manager, she and her team increased sales volume by nearly 20 percent. Amanda's boss was thrilled with Amanda's progression and gave her the freedom to decide exactly how she would achieve the goals that were set for her. Nearly three years after Amanda started her job, the dealership sold and a new general manager replaced Amanda's former boss. Not long after the new general manager started, Amanda's motivation started to decrease. Not only did her manager micromanage Amanda, which was not at all necessary, but he was also aggressive and demeaning in the way that he communicated with employees. Within a year, Amanda and numerous other high-performing employees left their jobs.

No organization or boss wants to demotivate their employees. Demotivation doesn't benefit anyone. It doesn't benefit organizations that lose institutional experience and have to spend more money on hiring and training new employees; it doesn't benefit bosses who end up missing key performance indicators due to employee absenteeism, disinterest, or disdain for their jobs; and it doesn't benefit employees who start to experience short-term and long-term symptoms of stress that can affect mental, physical, and emotional health.

We opened *The Demotivated Employee* with the contention that the issue isn't how to motivate employees; it's how to stop demotivating them. We also offered a different perspective regarding motivation based upon our professional experiences and empirical research. We then walked through the five sources of demotivation, which include individual differences, workplace stress, organizational culture, conflict between coworkers, and leadership style. Because each of these sources can cause employees to lose their motivation, it's important that leaders develop a collective understanding of the key aspects of each one, along with research-based actions that can be used to mitigate the negative consequences and to create a workplace environment that nurtures employee motivation.

In addition to sharing our professional experiences and research, we've included reflection and self-assessment as tools to help you develop a better understanding of yourself. Self-awareness is essential because it allows you to "know thyself" and can help to increase the efficacy of your workplace interactions. Equally important is deciding what steps you're going to take in order to apply this insight and learning. Taking action is key, because it's not enough to learn and discover. That's why we've encouraged you in a variety of ways, throughout the book, to identify action steps that you can take. You've likely figured out that we love storytelling. We believe there's immense value in reading about the experiences of others, imagining yourself in a similar situation and seeing how others have handled it. This can be instructive and help you to formulate your own strategy on how you might handle a similar situation as a leader. So we thought it would be fitting to share a final story with you about a leader who noticed that one of her employees was losing motivation and how she took action to turn things around.

Jacob was a steady performer who had been an analyst in the underwriting department for a mortgage company for the past eight years. Jacob was detail-oriented and knew the ins and outs of his job. He was an extrovert who was full of good ideas and shared them when asked. He was friendly and willing to help wherever needed. He was often praised by his peers for the quality of his work and how he genuinely cared for the employees on his team. Jacob was content in his role and wasn't really looking for an additional opportunity. Then, one day, his manager, Tonya, approached him about being promoted to a senior analyst, working on special projects that had more complexity. Jacob was surprised, nervous, and excited—all at the same time. After meeting with Tonya about the new role and responsibilities, Jacob agreed to the promotion. Even though he hadn't been looking for an opportunity, he was eager for the chance to grow and to have additional responsibility.

After a few weeks in his new role, Tonya noticed a change in Jacob. She noticed that he was spending a lot of time in his office and missing lunch breaks. There was a visible strain on his face and his friendly demeanor had been replaced by looks of frustration and complaints about how he was falling behind in his work. So Tonya stopped by Jacob's office to check in to see how things were going.

Jacob gave the pat response, "It's going fine." But Tonya recognized that Jacob was giving her a canned response. So she said, "Jacob, I noticed that you worked long hours last week and missed your lunch breaks. What can I do to help?"

While Jacob wasn't one to ask for help, he was feeling overwhelmed and began to open up to Tonya about the struggles he was having. Tonya listened and empathized with him. They talked in detail about where he was "drowning" and why he thought this was the case. Together, they came up with a game plan to help Jacob get on top of his workload. Tonya offered to help him with organizing his work by creating calendar blocks that would allow him to work uninterrupted. They also agreed to meet each Monday for a thirty-minute huddle to discuss what was on Jacob's desk for the week, any competing priorities, and a weekly work plan. Jacob was visibly relieved after the meeting and thanked Tonya for her help.

While his progress wasn't breakthrough, it was incremental. And this daily progress re-energized him, reduced his stress level, and reminded him of why he had chosen his career and why he had chosen the company.

As you read through this final example of workplace demotivation, what do you notice about the relationship between Jacob and Tonya and how their interactions impacted demotivation?

Did you notice how Tonya recognized Jacob was struggling with feelings of competence, in part because he was overwhelmed? As noted previously in our Chapter 3 discussion, it's not uncommon for employees to have these feelings when they're in a new role and getting up to speed. To help employees navigate their new reality, it's important that leaders notice and then partner with the employee to help them get up to speed. This goes a long way to reducing stress and helping the employee to get control over the work and become more comfortable with the demands. As noted in Chapter 4, decreasing Jacob's stress has tangible benefits for the company because he's less likely to be absent or quit and more likely to be productive and satisfied with his work, which contributes to developing affective commitment.

Did you notice the organizational culture? How would you describe it and what impact did it have on how Tonya handled the situation? We believe the mortgage firm's culture can best be described as clan. As discussed in Chapter 5, a clan culture is characterized by a supportive and family spirit where employees know their managers care about them. Tonya demonstrated her genuine care and concern for Jacob by reaching out to him and asking how she could help. While there's not explicit task conflict—Jacob and a coworker do not disagree over how the work should be done—it's evident that Jacob is struggling with figuring out how to best perform the tasks and fulfill responsibilities that are part of his senior analyst role. Tonya supports Jacob by "rolling up her sleeves," helping him to problem-solve and coming up with workable solutions that resolve

> EQUIPPING EMPLOYEES WITH THEIR OWN SKILLS TO RESOLVE CONFLICT CAN BE VERY EMPOWERING, ENABLING THEM TO FIGURE THINGS OUT IN THE FUTURE WITHOUT THE MANAGER'S ASSISTANCE.

the conflict he's experiencing. As noted in Chapter 6, equipping employees with their own skills to resolve conflict can be very empowering, enabling them to figure things out in the future without the manager's assistance.

Finally, in her leadership style, notice how she went to Jacob's office to talk to him. She didn't tell him to come to her. Instead, she was willing to go into his space and interact with him in a way that eliminated the sense of hierarchy that can be felt when employees have to go to the manager's office for a meeting to discuss an issue.

This likely helped to make Jacob, who wasn't inclined to ask for help, to be more comfortable and willing to share what was really going on. As noted in Chapter 7, it's important that leaders have the ability to flex their leadership style to match the situation they're facing. In this instance, we can see Tonya deploying a coaching style where she's investing time in Jacob, providing feedback, and working with him to identify the way forward. Given that Jacob has some holes in his motivation basket, it's important that Tonya is engaging in behaviors that will help Jacob repair the holes.

As you think about Jacob and Tonya's story and what you've learned in this book through our research and the lived experiences of others, it's our hope that you will take concrete action steps to determine what you can start doing in order to stop demotivating your employees.

Since you've taken the time to read this book, it's evident that you're interested in growing and developing yourself. One way to support that aspiration is to create a leadership development plan. This is a tool we use in the MBA program at Northwood University, and we've found that it's very useful to our students as they develop their leadership skills and behaviors.

LEADERSHIP DEVELOPMENT PLAN: GOAL PLANNING WORKSHEET

(*Reproduce worksheet as needed for each goal)

Identify One Specific Goal: Why is this important and what is the desired outcome for you?	
Benefits of Achieving Goal—What are the positive impacts to team and organizational success as a result of achieving this goal?	
Current Behavior—Describe the current behavior you wish to change or improve with this goal.	
Future Behavior—What is the desired behavior/actions you wish to start or improve to help you achieve your goal? Review the leadership behaviors in each chapter.	
Developmental Actions with Due Dates—What steps will you take to learn or improve the new, desired behaviors? What will it look like, and how are you going to do it?	
Feedback and Resources—What do you need from people? What other kinds of resources?	
Success Factors—How will you know you are making progress in a timely and accurate manner?	

(Source: Adapted from The Center for Faculty Excellence at the University of North Carolina)

You'll recall that at specific points within each of the chapters, we've attempted to tap into your self-awareness through reflection, assessment, and idea-sharing on leadership behaviors that will keep you from poking holes in your employee's motivation basket or help to repair them. Review those activities and identify at least one leadership goal that you want to pursue; you're always welcome to do more.

So, maybe you'll decide to create a goal in relation to the person who's struggling with motivation that you identified in Chapter 3. Or perhaps your work environment is stressful, and after reading Chapter 4, you realize that it's important to create a healthier work environment. Or after reading Chapter 5, you recognize that your employees are becoming demotivated by something that exists in the organizational culture and you want to set a related goal. You get to decide what goal is most meaningful for you in your leadership journey at this point in time. What's important is that you set a goal and then complete the worksheet. We encourage you to not only engage in thorough self-assessment and reflection on your strengths and weaknesses as a leader, but we also encourage you to get objective input from three people who have knowledge of and experience with your performance.

At the beginning of *The Demotivated Employee*, we stated that our goal was to train you to look for the five sources of demotivation on a consistent basis as you work with employees. In doing so, you will be able to resolve any issues that may arise in a timely manner, so that your employees can bounce back quickly and return to being very productive and highly engaged.

Now that you've read our book, it's our hope that you'll share what you've learned with others in your organization to solve the motivation crisis that's plaguing business.

APPENDIX

Use this appendix to reflect on the actions that you might take to significantly impact employee demotivation.

CHAPTER 3: LEADERSHIP ACTIONS THAT IMPACT INDIVIDUAL SOURCES OF DEMOTIVATION

1. Interact frequently with each of your employees.
2. Consider matching employee personality and disposition in hiring and staffing decisions.
3. Include personality testing as part of the employee development process.
4. Invest in employee development training to help employees build competence.
5. When "stretching" employees outside of their comfort zones, use frequent coaching and feedback to prevent motivational slumping.
6. Clarify expectations and assumptions directly with employees to avoid misunderstandings.
7. Pay attention to body language to assess motivational changes in employees.
8. Talk directly with employees about their motivation, rather than talking about them.

CHAPTER 4: LEADERSHIP ACTIONS TO REDUCE THE DEMOTIVATING EFFECT OF WORKPLACE STRESS

1. Engage employees from the beginning of a potentially stressful situation.
2. Acknowledge the stress impact (rather than pretending it doesn't exist).
3. Monitor demand levels of the work, specifically for high-performing employees.
4. Provide frequent opportunities for employees to engage in stress-relieving activities.
5. Step up and pitch in to complete tasks that add stress to employees.
6. Remove obstacles that may increase stress for employees.
7. Increase predictability in processes and communication patterns to help employees achieve a sense of control over the stress.
8. Celebrate successes in terms of effort, attitude, and endurance during stressful times.

CHAPTER 5: LEADERSHIP ACTIONS TO PREVENT A DEMOTIVATING ORGANIZATIONAL CULTURE

1. Assess the culture of your organization and the impact that the culture is having on employees.
2. Engage employees in helping you understand their expectations and preferences for organizational culture.
3. Engage other managers and leaders in the organization, as well as stakeholders such as customers or vendors, to understand how they view the culture of the organization as well as the subculture of your department.
4. Consider the impact of how information flows through your

organization, and examine if this matches the needs of employees.

5. Examine how your leadership style and expectations for employees in your department match (or differ from) the overall culture of the organization.

6. If your department requires a different culture than the current one, make adjustments to build the culture that works best within the department.

7. Celebrate your organizational culture within your own department.

8. Dare to change your organizational culture if the one you have is demotivating your employees.

CHAPTER 6: LEADERSHIP ACTIONS TO REDUCE THE DEMOTIVATING EFFECT OF WORKPLACE CONFLICT

1. Provide opportunities for employees to learn about their own conflict management styles and work toward developing a wider range of approaches.

2. Assess your own approach to managing conflict and the impact this has on the employees in your group.

3. Help the team to develop agreements about how to gain value from differences and address the conflict that comes from diverse perspectives.

4. Rather than separating employees who appear to struggle to work together, create more opportunities for collaboration and facilitate agreements to help them recognize the value in working together.

5. Help employees establish norms to keep disagreements focused on the work rather than on emotions and personal differences.

6. Establish an environment of inclusion rather than foster exclusive

relationships within the team.

7. Provide opportunities for the team to build social cohesiveness beyond the work tasks.

8. Establish strong feedback skills so that individuals can effectively communicate concerns with each other directly.

CHAPTER 7: LEADERSHIP ACTIONS THAT IMPACT DEMOTIVATION OF EMPLOYEES OVERALL

1. Explain the Why
2. Communicate Frequently and Clearly
3. Invite Input and Opinions
4. Provide Effective Feedback and Coaching
5. Remove Obstacles
6. Develop a Range of Leadership Styles

OUR SERVICES

THE LEADERSHIP DOCTORS: CREATING GREAT WORKPLACES THROUGH LEADERSHIP DEVELOPMENT

The Leadership Doctors is a consulting group that was formed by Dr. Cathy Bush and Dr. Tara Peters. We are dedicated to helping leaders create great workplaces. Dr. Cathy earned a PhD in Industrial/Organizational Psychology, and Dr. Tara earned a PhD in Educational Leadership, which, combined with our experiences working with thousands of leaders over the past few decades, make us uniquely qualified to help your organization. We are excited to bring our experience and enthusiasm to any organization that is striving to help leaders learn how to create a great place for people to come to work and a place where customers enjoying doing business.

We offer the following services:

LEADERSHIP DEVELOPMENT TEAMS

This is a unique process model to increase the likelihood that current and emergent leaders will go beyond learning a few new ideas about leading others and will actually be able to practice and grow their leadership skills. We call this the Leadership Development Team

Process. It consists of a series of activities in the real workplace, along with several short leadership development meetings with small groups of leaders in the same organization. These small groups of leaders serve as a support system for each other while everyone learns new ideas and practices new leadership behaviors. We can customize this process for various leadership topics and skills and typically work with groups for a span of three to six months.

EXECUTIVE COACHING

If you are interested in working on your own leadership development, we also offer one-on-one coaching that will include some discovery of your strengths and challenges, some exploration and practice of new leadership behaviors, and some action planning to help you make sustainable changes in your approach to leading others.

LEARN MORE

Visit www.theleadershipdoctors.com and use the contact form to reach us directly.

We also invite you to subscribe to our YouTube Channel, our newsletter, or check us out on social media. You can find links to all of these options by going to our website www.theleadershipdoctors.com.

REFERENCES

Allen, Natalie J., and John P. Meyer. 1996. "Affective, Continuance, and Normative Commitment to the Organization: An Examination of Construct Validity." *Journal of Vocational Behavior*, 49: 252–276.

Bandura, Albert. 1977. *Social Learning Theory*. Englewood Cliffs, NJ: Prentice-Hall.

Bass, Bernard M. 1990. "From Transactional to Transformational Leadership: Learning to Share the Vision. *Organizational Dynamics*, 18(3): 19–31.

Blanchard, Kenneth H., Patricia Zigarmi, and Drea Zigarmi. 2013. *Leadership and the One Minute Manager: Increasing Effectiveness Through Situational Leadership® II*. New York, NY: Harper Collins.

Buckingham, Marcus, and Curt Coffman. 1999. *First, Break All the Rules: What the World's Greatest Managers Do Differently.* New York: Simon and Schuster.

Cameron, Kim S., and Robert E. Quinn. 2011. *Diagnosing and Changing Organizational Culture: Based on the Competing Values Framework*. San Francisco. Jossey-Bass.

Chartered Institute for Personnel and Development. 2015. *Getting under the Skin of Workplace Conflict: Tracing the Experiences of Employees.* http://www.cipd.co.uk/binaries/getting-under-skin-workplace-conflict_2015-tracing-experiences-employees.pdf.

Costa, Paul T., and Robert R. McCrae. 1992. *The NEO-PI Personality Inventory.* Odessa, FL: Psychological Assessment Resources.

Davis, Albie M. 2015. "When Webb Met Follett: Negotiation Theory and the Race to the Moon." *Negotiation Journal*, 31(3): 267–283. https://doi-org.librarydb.northwood.edu:2443/10.1111/nejo.12094.

Deci, Edward L. 1971. "Effects of externally mediated rewards on intrinsic motivation." *Journal of Personality and Social Psychology*, 18(1): 105–115.

Gallup. 2017a. *State of the American Workplace—Employee engagement Insight for US Business Leaders.* Washington, DC: Gallup, Inc.

Gallup. 2017b. *State of the Global Workplace.* Washington, DC: Gallup, Inc.

Gallup. 2017c. *State of the American Workplace Report—A Closer Look at the 12 Elements of Engagement.* Washington, DC: Gallup, Inc.

Goh, Joel, Jeffrey Pfeffer, and Stefanos Zenios. 2016. "The Relationship between Workplace Stressors and Mortality and Health Costs in the United States." *Management Science*, 62(2): 608–628.

Goleman, Daniel. 2000. "Leadership that gets results." *Harvard Business Review*. March-April.

Hellebuyck, Michele et al. 2017. *Mind the workplace.* Mental Health America. https://www.mhanational.org/sites/default/files/Mind%20the%20Workplace%20-%20MHA%20Workplace%20Health%20Survey%202017%20FINAL.PDF.

Herzberg, Frederick. 2008. *One More Time: How Do You Motivate Employees?* Boston: Harvard Business School Publishing.

Joni, Saj-nicole and Damon Beyer. 2009. "How to Pick a Good Fight." *Harvard Business Review*, December.

Judge, Timothy A., Edwin A. Locke, and Cathy C. Durham. 1997. "The Dispositional Causes of Job Satisfaction: A Core Self-Evaluation Approach." *Research in Organizational Behavior,* 19: 151–188.

Kazimoto, Paluku. 2013. "Analysis of Conflict Management and Leadership for Organizational Change. *International Journal of Research in Social Sciences*, 3(1): 16–25.

Kotter, John P. 1996. *Leading Change.* Cambridge: Harvard Business Review Press.

Locke, Edwin A., and Gary P. Latham. 1990. *A Theory of Goal Setting and Task Performance.* Englewood Cliffs, NJ: Prentice-Hall.

Maslow, Abraham H. 1943. "A theory of human motivation." *Psychological Review*, 50: 370–396.

McGregor, Douglas. 1960. *The Human Side of Enterprise.* New York: McGraw-Hill.

Mowday, Richard T., Lyman W. Porter, and Richard M. Steers. 1982. *Employee-Organization Linkages: The Psychology of Commitment.* New York: Academic Press.

Pink, Daniel H. 2009. *Drive: The Surprising Truth About What Motivates Us.* New York: Penguin Random House.

Porath, Christine. 2016. *Mastering Civility: A Manifesto for the Workplace.* New York: Grand Central Publishing.

Posthuma, Richard A., Carl P. Maertz, and James B. Dworkin. 2007. "Procedural Justice's Relationship with Turnover: Explaining Past Inconsistent Findings." *Journal of Organizational Behavior*, 28(4): 381–398.

Robbins, Stephan, and Timothy A. Judge. 2015. *Organizational Behavior.* 16th Edition. Boston: Pearson.

Schein, Edgar. 2016. *Organizational Culture and Leadership*, 5th edition. San Francisco. Jossey-Bass.

Schwartz, Barry. 2015. *Why We Work.* New York: TED Books: Simon & Schuster, Inc.

Selye, Hans. 1979. *The Stress of My Life: A Scientist's Memoirs.* New York, NY: Van Nostrand Reinhold Company.

Sinek, Simon. 2009. *Start with Why.* New York: The Penguin Group.

Skinner, B.F. 1969. *Contingencies of Reinforcement: A Theoretical Analysis.* New York: Appleton-Century-Crofts.

Society for Human Resource Management. 2017. *Managing workplace conflict.* https://www.shrm.org/resourcesandtools/tools-and-samples/toolkits/pages/managingworkplaceconflict.aspx.

Spencer, Robin W. 2013. "Work Is Not a Game." *Research Technology Management*, 56(6): 59–60.

Spitzer, Dean R. 1995. "The Seven Deadly Demotivators." *Management Review*, 84(11): 56.

Zhao, Hao, Sandy J. Wayne, Brian C. Glibkowski, and Jesus Bravo. 2007. "The Impact of Psychological Contract Breach on Work-Related Outcomes." *Personnel Psychology* 60(3): 647–680.